I0832069

"Recluse Island," (near Bolton,) Lake George.

LAKE GEORGE:

Its Scenes and Characteristics, with Glimpses of the Olden Times.

TO WHICH IS ADDED SOME ACCOUNT OF TICONDEROGA, WITH A DESCRIPTION OF THE ROUTE TO

Schroon Lake and the Adirondacks.

WITH AN APPENDIX,
CONTAINING NOTES ON LAKE CHAMPLAIN.

With Illustrations.

By B. F. De Costa.

NEW YORK:
ANSON D. F. RANDOLPH,
770 Broadway.
1868.

PREFACE.

THIS book is designed to convey, in a compact form, all that general readers may desire to know about Lake George.

The author was originally attracted to the subject by its rare charms, and afterwards persuaded to throw his thoughts into the present shape, for the reason that a book of this kind was actually needed; especially as Lake George has suffered so much at the hands of magazine writers and others, who have done little more than to transcribe popular errors.

In preparing this work the author has sifted out the legends from the facts, which, in the history of this Lake, are quite as romantic as any fiction, and has endeavored to base his statements on original authorities.

That no lake in America has greater claims to consideration, is abundantly proved by the increasing throngs of visitors who assemble at the Lake every summer. This is pre-eminently "Health's cheerful haunt." The pure air, the lovely scenes, and the numberless localities consecrated by song and story, form an attraction to which few persons could be insensible.

The tourist at the Lake will find this work a complete guide, and by following the author's suggestions he will gain an introduction to every point of interest.

The concluding chapter is chiefly the work of one of the author's friends. It will afford all the information needed in regard to the new stage-route to Schroon Lake and the Adirondacks, which connects Lake George with that entire region.

The author acknowledges his indebtedness to various persons for valuable suggestions and historical information; and among others to Mr. JOHN GILMARY SHEA; but especially to MR. WILLIAM KELBY, who has proved indefatigable in his efforts to search out and verify facts in the history of Lake George.

Thanks are also due to MR. S. R. STODDARD, of Glen's Falls, N. Y., for the use of valuable photographic views of the Lake — views which deserve to be generally known, and which are executed, like all the works of this enthusiastic photographer, with great fidelity and skill.

STUYVESANT SQUARE,

NEW YORK, 1868.

Contents.

Chapter I. . . . . L'Overture.
Chapter II. . . . . Down the Lake.
Chapter III. . . . The Lake in the Seasons.
Chapter IV. . . . . . . Among the Islands.
Chapter V. . . . . In General.
Chapter VI. . . . . Colonial Days.
Chapter VII. . . . . Colonial Days.
Chapter VIII. . . . Revolutionary Scenes.
Chapter IX. . . . . Ticonderoga.
Chapter X. . . . . . Schroon Lake and the Adirondacks.

LAKE GEORGE.

L'OVERTURE.

CHAPTER I.

> Scenes must be beautiful, which, daily viewed,
> Please daily, and whose novelty survives
> Long knowledge and the scrutiny of years. — *Cowper.*

SITUATION — EXTENT — GLEN'S FALLS — FIRST VIEW — PROSPECT MOUNTAIN — BLACK MOUNTAIN — THE BOLTON VIEW — HISTORIC ASSOCIATIONS.

FIRST we must speak of the situation of Lake George, which lies at the head of a valley of the St. Lawrence extending southward through Vermont and New York, and reaching nearly to the Hudson River. It is about thirty-five miles long, and from one mile to four miles wide. The broadest part is found about eight miles from Ticonderoga, while it attains its greatest depth at a point four miles farther north. It is elevated, probably, about three hundred feet above the sea; and, according to fair estimates, it must stand two hundred and forty feet above the level of Lake Champlain, the receptacle of its surplus water, which passes through a creek, and flows over two picturesque falls. Surrounded on all sides, except at the outlet, by beautiful hills, and mountains of primitive rock, it receives from their springs and brooks an unfailing supply of water that is sufficiently sparkling and pure to justify the name — St. Sacrament — which the lake originally received.

At some remote period, this whole region was swept over by a great deluge which left the country far and wide covered with loose earth and gravel, and gave to the lake a floor of beautiful white sand. This, in connection with the crystal purity of the water, renders objects visible at a considerable depth.

Only a small portion of the lake is seen at a single view. There is no broad and striking expanse of water. This lake (like Como and Windermere) assumes more of the character of a noble river flanked by highlands. Winding sweetly on its way among the verdant hills, it gradually unfolds its wealth of beauty, surprising and delighting the tourist at every advance by some new and exquisite scene.

In approaching the lake from Albany, the tourist takes the Saratoga railroad, and, passing north, alights at Moreau station, whence he goes on fourteen miles by coach, or else he continues on to Whitehall to take the steamer for Ticonderoga, and approaches the lake from the north. Most persons, however, prefer the round trip, thus going by one route and returning by the other.

In taking the first-mentioned route, the traveller will do well to secure a seat upon the top of the coach, and thus be the better prepared to get the full benefit of the journey. The first four miles take him over a somewhat soft and hilly road to the thriving village of Glen's Falls, leaving Fort Edward in the distance on the right. Descending the hill at that place, a full view of the Falls of the Hudson bursts upon the sight. The river makes a descent of about sixty feet, in a succession of falls. When the stream is full the sight is magnificient and one that well repays the trouble of a journey. The bed and walls of the river are composed of blue, fossiliferous limestone, and the scenery is bold and striking. The admirers of Cooper must not fail to explore the falls and visit the cave under the rocks below, where the novelist lays the most thrilling scenes depicted in *The Last of the Mohicans.* It was in this cave that Hayward and Cora found refuge; where David struck his pitch-pipe, and sang the "Isle of White" to the chiming of the music of the falls.

Leaving Glen's Falls, the coach rolls on through a beautiful undulating region, whose scenery cannot fail to charm the eye. Soon after leaving Glen's Falls, French Mountain rises to view; and, after passing the Notch, at about three miles from the lake, is seen the monument to Colonel Williams, who was killed in the

Battle of Lake George, fought on this spot, Sept. 8, 1755. This monument was erected by the Alumni of Williams College, upon the rough boulder upon which, it is *said*, Williams stood when he received his death-wound.[1] A little further on may be seen "Bloody Pond," where Baron Dieskau's troops halted after

BLOODY POND.

their defeat, and where, at sunset, they were again attacked, and routed with much slaughter, and, it is said, mingled their blood with the water of this shallow pond, which in the season is covered with beautiful white lilies.

(1) — Col. Williams was buried near where he fell. His grave was opened about thirty years ago, and not long since his skull was in the possession of a physician in South Carolina.

About half a mile from the village of Caldwell, the south, or upper end of Lake George, comes in sight, glittering among the verdant hills like a sea of glass. This view is one of extreme beauty, yet in the course of his rambles down the lake, the traveller will obtain others that are finer.

In order to obtain an extended view of the lake, it is necessary to climb some one of the mountains on the border. A fine view may be had from the eminence called Rattlesnake Cobble, which rises south of the village of Caldwell. A mountain road leaves the highway opposite the Fort William Henry Hotel, and winds around the base of the mountain, through a fine wood, enabling the tourist to walk easily half way up the ascent. He then leaves the road and moves directly toward the summit, and, in the absence of a path, climbs over fallen trees, ledges and loose rocks, which task a strong man's strength. On the top of the Cobble there is an open space in the woods, which forms a beautiful out-look upon the lake. Here the village of Caldwell is seen directly below our feet, while half of the lake, dotted with green isles, and fenced in by mountains, stretches away before the sight until lost in the haze, out of which Black Mountain looms, apparently barring the way. The view from this point is one that delights the eye; and though the neighboring and much loftier Prospect Mountain, with its beaten path, is oftener climbed, it can afford no such satisfactory view of the lake. The glimpse gained from that mountain may be far more grand, but it is certainly not superior in beauty. Indeed, at the present time, the view from the *apex* of Prospect Mountain is wholly obstructed by the trees. It is found, when reached, to be a place

> "Where to the north, pine trees in prospect rise;
> Where to the east, pine trees assail the skies;
> Where to the west, pine trees obstruct the view;
> Where to the south, pine trees forever grow!"

In fact the climber sees nothing else. Yet, by descending a few rods, he will find an opening where he may get a tolerable glimpse of the country towards the east and south.

Three hours will suffice for the trip up Cobble Hill, which may be safely achieved, notwithstanding the stories that he will hear about snakes; while to ascend Prospect Mountain will ordinarily consume the greater portion of a day. But no one should leave the lake without ascending both. Nor would it be altogether unprofitable to climb the French Mountain, on the east side of the lake, above which the traveller first beholds the morning sun.

A still more lovely view may be had at Bolton, ten miles down the lake, from an eminence also called Prospect Mountain, where the air

> "Nimbly and sweetly recommends itself
> Unto our gentle senses."

The Bolton view has a wider range, and is more comprehensive than that at the head of the lake, in addition to being more attractive. Here we take our second lesson in the geography of the lake, and, overlooking the Narrows, (which in early times was called the *First* Narrows, to distinguish them from the Narrows at the outlet), we get a glimpse of the region beyond. Seen from this point, the lake loses the crowded aspect which it wears while we are upon its shores, and the islands appear reduced in size. Black Mountain, however, affords a view which, for grandeur, eclipses everything else.

About three miles north of Fourteen Mile Island, in a small clearing, stands an old house used in the winter by the Black Mountain lumbermen. This is the point of departure in making the ascent. Taking one of the rough roads used in winter in hauling logs, we follow it for about three miles, which brings us to a pond, situated a mile from the summit, and which in the summer is flecked with lilies. At this point we turn to the left and clamber on as best we may. Up we go along the dry bed of winter torrents, and over loose debris and huge rocks magnificently embossed with rich lichens. Here and there in a crevice may be found a spring at which we can quench our thirst, while beautiful harebells delight the eye. This mountain does not afford any opportunities for the study of Alpine flora, though the botanist may occasionally find the sand-wort (*Greenlandica arenaria*), which bears a pretty white flower worth preserving.

This, like all mountains, is very deceptive. In a transparent atmosphere its summit does not appear very distant, yet as we go forward, it recedes and beckons us on and up, while occasionally we lose sight of it altogether. It is very provoking sometimes to be obliged to scramble for two hours over the rocks to reach a point that you expected to reach in a few minutes. Yet the journey is not without its rich compensations, and, as we mount up, we find ourselves slowly rising into a new world. Finally, we stand on the bare and desolate peak of Black Mountain, where the eye sweeps the entire horizon, and sees the green hills everywhere rolling like billows, while the lake reposes in the vale below, mute and motionless as a silver sea. This is a place eminently calculated to inspire lofty sentiments. With the poet one may say:

> "There as thou standst
> The haunts of men below thee, and around
> The mountain summits, thy expanding heart
> Shall feel a kindred with that loftier world
> To which thou art translated, and partake
> The enlargement of thy vision."

Here, however, few persons rise in their inspiration above the need of bodily nourishment, as the remains of numerous bottles abundantly testify.

From this elevation the scene is one of great variety. Besides the lake at our feet, Champlain stretches away toward the north; in the south may be seen the Hudson, glittering like a silver thread; in the northwest are the Adirondacks; and away in the east are the Green Mountains, with Camel's Hump. It is interesting to watch the steamer Minnehaha running up the lake from Ticonderoga, winding her way among the numerous islands, and leaving a trail of light on the surface of the calm lake.

In visiting Black Mountain, strangers should take a guide and start early in the day, or else prepare to spend the night somewhere on its side.

But, although so much has been said of the mountain-views, we must not forget the beautiful walks that are to be found among the wild old woods on the hill-sides and along the shores. In the language of another, we may say:

"Nor is the stately scene without
  Its sweet, secluded treasures,
Where hearts that there the crowd may find
  Their own exclusive pleasures;
Deep, charming shades for pensive thought,
  The hours to wear away in,
And vaulted isles of whispering pines,
  For lover's feet to stray in."

Long ago the beauty of Lake George began to attract the attention of travellers, many of whom were foreigners. It was even then the general opinion, that no lake exceeded it in loveliness. By some visitors, it was called "the Como of America," and others compared it to the lakes of Westmoreland and some of the Scotch lakes; while all agreed that it must eventually become a popular resort. The prediction has been more than justified by the thousands of tourists who now annually visit Lake George.

This lake is adorned with no ivied ruin or lordly hall. Besides Caldwell, (a summer convenience, more for use than ornament,) there are only four villages, — Bolton, Dresden, Hague, and Ticonderoga. Here and there the boatman finds a farm-house or cottage, but he may sail for miles among certain districts, without seeing a sign of human life. And yet there is no lack of antiquity. Among the lofty hills he will find peaks that were laid bare before Eden bloomed, towers more ancient than Babel, and nature-carved crags that rejoiced in the sun's warm rays before Memnon began to sing.

As with the scenery so with its historic associations, in which no lake can be richer. There is hardly a spot, either on land or water, that has not been the scene of some warlike exploit or heroic adventure. Forming in colonial times a part of the great highway between Canada and New York, it was often the chosen battle-ground of the French and English, who, in connection with hostile Indian tribes, waged a barbarous war on each other. Often was the lake traversed by the soldier, the savage, and the monk. Hither came the brave Montcalm, the pious Father Joques, the good Roubaud, Rigaud, St. Ours, and Courcelles, together with Abercrombie, Howe, Lord Amherst, Putnam, Rogers the Ranger, Johnson, Williams, "King Hendrick," and Stark, and a multitude of others who are invested with historic renown. The story of their deeds contains all the elements of romance. Cooper in his novels has invested the lake with a thrilling interest, but the literal history is ofttimes stranger than the overwrought fiction.

It is also interesting to be reminded of the fact that the French pushed their discoveries in this direction in early times, and that Champlain, who heard of the Hudson River through the Indians, started on his way thither, intending to go by Lake St. Sacrament, about the same time that Hendrick Hudson was sailing up to Albany, which was four years before the Dutch took possession of New York, and eleven years before the English Puritans landed on Plymouth Rock.

In times of peace the Indian hunted the deer which abounded in the woods, or, gliding over the waters in his canoe, darted his spear at the trout. But when the signal for war was given, the lake became alive with armed men all eager for the fight. Then those sweet and tranquil scenes upon which the tourist now delights to gaze were obscured by the smoke of battle, and the solitudes echoed with the rattle of the musket and the boom of artillery. Rogers and Putnam both traversed the lake, with cannon mounted on their boats, which scattered the Indian canoes in fragments on the water; and in the winter they traversed the ice on skates, and, after the fight, carried their wounded home on sleds. The imaginative mind can easily re-animate the lake with the splendid armies of

Abercrombie, Amherst, and Montcalm, numbering from nine to sixteen thousand men each, and sailing in boats and batteaux, marshalled in beautiful array, with all the pomp and circumstance of war. How peaceful it appears to-day at the head of the lake around the ruins of Fort George, and the grass-grown

FORT GEORGE.

site of Fort William Henry! Yet here, through long and bloody wars, the cross of St. George waved defiance to the Lilies of France. Here forts and palisades went up, opposing trenches were dug, and mines sprung. Here the iron-mouthed cannon from the narrow embrasures of Munro, belched out death by day, while the huge bomb with its fiery trail came shrieking from the camp of Montcalm by night. Here, too, was the scene of the massacre of the English by the French Indians cf St. Francis. But now all signs of bloodshed and strife have passed away. The hapless victims are forever at rest; and the descendants of the Abenakis, from the ancient village of their fathers, now unconsciously pitch their summer tents, and pursue the harmless trade of the basket-maker, over their graves.

DOWN THE LAKE.

CHAPTER II.

The crowded steamer leaves the village pier;
Its paddles splash; it flaunts a gaudy flag:
And brazen music loudens into noise.

THE START — FRENCH MOUNTAIN — THE ISLANDS — BOLTON — THE NARROWS — TONGUE MOUNTAIN — BLACK MOUNTAIN — BUCK MOUNTAIN — SABBATH DAY POINT — HAGUE — FRIENDS' POINT — ANTHONY'S NOSE — ROGERS' SLIDE — PRISONERS' ISLAND.

THE tourist, in order to view the lake, will find it necessary to pass over its entire length in the steamer, which runs regularly to Ticonderoga, going down in the morning and returning in the afternoon.

Leaving the little quay at Fort William Henry Hotel, the Minnehaha glides out into the centre of the lake, leaving behind a long line of foam. The high, wood-crowned mountain on the east side is French Mountain. It terminates in the beautiful point of land called Plum's Point. Two miles down the lake, on the west side, close to the shore, is the first island which we pass. It is called Tea Island,

TEA ISLAND.

and is a perfect gem. In 1828 a "Tea-house"[1] was kept there to accommodate visitors, which fact accounts for its present name.

About two miles farther on is Diamond Island. An account of its early use by Burgoyne, as a military depot, and of the defeat of Colonel Brown at this place, will be found in the chapters relating to the history of the lake. When the country was first settled, the island was overrun with rattlesnakes. One writer says, that the people seldom ventured upon it. Anbury[2] writes, on very good authority, that, before the Revolution, "A batteau, in sailing up the lake, overset near Diamond Island, and, among other things, it

(1) — Stewart's Trav., Vol. i., p. 121.
(2) — Anbury's Trav., Vol. i., p. 385.

contained several hogs, which swam to the shore, as did the Canadians, who were rowing. The latter, apprehensive of the rattlesnakes, climbed up trees for the night, and the next morning, observing a batteau, they hailed the people in it who took them in." It is called Diamond Island on account of the beautiful quartz crystals obtained here. Silliman, who was here in 1819, says: "The crystals are hardly surpassed by any in the world for transparency and perfection of form. They are, as usual, the six-sided prism, and are frequently terminated at both ends by six-sided pyramids. These last, of course, must be found loose, or, at least, not adhering to any rock; those which are broken off have necessarily only one pyramid."[1]

Writing at this time, he says: "There is a solitary miserable cottage upon this island, from which we saw the smoke ascending; — a woman who lives in it, is facetiously called, 'The Lady of the Lake,' but, probably, no Malcolm Græme and Rhoderick Dhu will ever contend on her account."[2]

In 1821 he visited the lake again, when he remarks of Diamond Island: "This small island, scarcely covering the area of a common kitchen garden, is inhabited by a family who occupy a small but comfortable house, and constantly explore the rocks for crystals. . . . At present, they are scarcely obtained at all, except by breaking the rocks."[3]

(1)—Silliman's Trav., p. 153. (2)—ib. p. 152. (3)—ib. p. 168.

Near by, on the shore, there was a place called Diamond Point, where crystals were also obtained by the same man — an Indian named Sampson Paul. It is said that he once killed an immense panther at this place, as the animal was coming out of the lake benumbed with cold. The little bay beyond this point is Montcalm's Bay.

Beyond Plum's Point is Dunham's Bay, where some say Colonel Brown landed after his defeat at Diamond Island. One mile beyond, are the Three Sisters, though properly there are only two islands; and a little way east is Long Island, where Rogers camped one winter's night in 1758, after having been defeated by the French. In the bay, farther to the right, is the hotel called "Trout Pavilion," one resort of those who are fond of fine fish. As we pass on to Bolton, which is ten miles from Caldwell, we leave on the west side the islands called The Three Brothers. To the right is a large and heavily wooded island, called Dome Island, on account of its resemblance to a dome.

West of Dome Island is Recluse Island,[1] a lovely spot, commanding a fine view of the lake in all directions. This island is owned by Rufus Wattles, Esq.,

(1) — This is the island which, in January of 1868, was reported as sunk by an earthquake, and which, consequently, became so famous in the newspapers. It stands to-day as fair as ever, and will last as long as the lake, it being nothing less than a part of the lake's bed, which was lifted up into its present position during that dim antiquity to which the formation of this region must be referred.

of New York, who has here erected the only private residence yet to be found on the islands of the lake. It is a neat cottage, embowered among the trees, where a genial hospitality is gracefully dispensed.

On the sides of this island, facing the Narrows and Bolton, are the remains of some earthworks, which were probably erected by Abercrombie's forces, who, in 1758, were stationed on the lake. Near by, is an islet, often called Sloop Island, or Ship Island. In sailing down the lake, it appears in the distance like a small ship under sail. In 1851, it was visited by *Parodi*, the famous singer, who erected a rude cross, which still remains. Hence the island has sometimes been called by her name.

The steamer now heads in for the landing at Bolton, three-fourths of a mile distant, and one of the most charming parts of the lake. After touching at the landing, the Minnehaha starts for Fourteen Mile Island, which is four miles from Bolton, and located at the foot of Shelving Rock, on the right of the entrance to the Narrows. As we pass towards this spot, we leave Green Island on the left, beyond which, in the mouth of Northwest Bay, is the spot called, (with little taste or reason,) Hog Island. Directly in front is that beautiful elevation, called, from its shape, Tongue Mountain, and which, for a distance of six miles, forms the east side of Northwest Bay. As we approach Fourteen Mile Island, we get a just view of the Narrows. At this point the sides of the lake approach each other, and the space between is nearly filled up with clusters of islands, of various shapes and sizes, so that the steamer is obliged to wind carefully through. At a distance no passage can be seen, and

THE NARROWS.

the islands, covered with foliage, resemble a tongue of land, stretching across the lake, forming what often appears like an impassible barrier. At first, we look in vain for islands and a passage through. So it was on our last trip down the lake; but, on a nearer approach, the passage widened, and the little rifts in the woods, here and there, opened like celestial gates. Then

> "The shaggy mound no longer stood
> Emerging from entangled wood;
> But, wave-encircled, seemed to float,
> Like castle girdled with its moat:
> Yet broader floods extending still
> Divide them from the parent hill,
> Till each, retiring, claims to be,
> An islet in an inland sea."

But before going through, we stop at the landing, and have time to observe the beauty of the place and its rare adaptation as a summer resort. This site has advantages that are found nowhere else on the lake, and travellers who have the time will find it much to their advantage to spend some days here. Note also the group of islands called the Hen and Chickens, which lie near the east shore. On the west side, close by Tongue Mountain, is an island, the character of which may be gathered from its name, — Flea Island.

In passing through the Narrows, we find ourselves in the very heart of the lake, surrounded on every side by scenes that delight the eye. Black Mountain looms up directly before us. According to barometrical calculations, it is 2,878 feet above tide water, and is the highest mountain near the lake. It is banded around its sides with alternate lines of maple, pine, and birch, which thin out by degrees as they rise, until, two-thirds of the way up, the bare rocks chiefly appear, sentinelled here and there by a few dead trunks, while the top of the mountain stands out completely divested of verdure, and dark, threatening, and bare. The view from the summit is one of much grandeur. It is readily ascended with the aid of a guide. Around its scarred and rifted sides, often swept by fire, we see the work of time and weather, which

> " Down the lake in masses, threw
> Crags, knolls, and mounds confusedly hurl'd,
> The fragments of an earlier world."

The next islands to be noted are the Hatchet Islands, so called, from an Indian hatchet once found there. On the west, in the curved side of Tongue Mountain, close to the shore, nearer than the steamer usually goes, is a *double* echo, the sounds made there being repeated from two distinct quarters at the same instant.

On the west shore, farther on, is Half-Way Island, which marks the centre of the lake, being half way to Ticonderoga. Beyond Black Mountain, is next seen the Sugar Loaf, a spur of the former mountain, which now loses the symmetrical and imposing aspect that it presented from the Narrows, and seems to sink down, at the same time taking the appearance of a formless mass of rock, scooped out into deep ravines. Some persons fancy that in this vicinity they are able to detect a form in the north part of the mountain, which resembles an elephant's back, and hence it has sometimes been called Elephant's Ridge. Along the base of this mountain, may be seen the Floating Battery Islands. Opposite the Ridge is Harbor Island, the scene of Montcalm's first skirmish with the English. Next to it is Vicar's Island. On the right appears the little hamlet of Dresden, nestling in Bosom Bay. On the west is Buck Mountain, about eight hundred feet high, the side of which towards the Lake forms a sort of palisade. At one time, the deer were extremely plenty in this entire neighborhood. In 1802, Dr. Dwight, the grave divine, joined in the hunt, and captured a deer in the lake. The deer are usually hunted by dogs and driven into the water, where they are captured or killed. Buck Mountain received its name from the fact, that a buck, pursued by a hunter and his dogs, leaped from the precipice overhanging the lake, and was literally impaled alive on a sharp-pointed tree projecting below. Silliman, when on the lake, saw the man who drove the buck. Chasing the animal out of the woods, toward the open place which looks down at such a tremendous height upon the lake below, he believed that, with the help of his hounds, he was sure of his game. From afar,

> "The hunter marked that mountain high,
> The lone lake's western boundary,
> And deemed the stag must turn to bay,
> Where that huge rampart barred the way:
> Already, glorying in his prize,
> Measured his antlers with his eyes;
> For the death-wound and death-halloo,
> Muster'd his breath, his whinyard drew."

But he was disappointed at last, for the poor beast, now driven to desperation, had less fear of the precipice than of the dogs, and, reaching the brink, sprang forward into the air, and descending, met his cruel fate upon a sharp tree below.

As we sail on, Black Mountain rises behind us, and begins to assume the symmetry and commanding height which it completely loses while the traveller is sailing under its brow. The next place, on the west side of the lake, is the projecting tongue of land known as Sabbath Day Point. This name was given to the spot at an early day, though for what reason it is impossible now to say. Perhaps it was on account of the general aspect of peace which usually prevails. Magazine writers and others[1] say, that the place was so called by Abercrombie, in 1758, when, as they aver, he halted here on Sunday morning to refresh his troops, before proceeding to attack Ticonderoga. But a reference to the almanac shows that it was on a Wednesday, and not on a Sunday, that he landed here. Nor, as others say, was the name given by Lord Amherst the year following. In fact, the French officers of Montcalm's army, in their official reports, dated one year before Abercrombie came to the lake, call the place Sabbath Day Point, a name by which it was at that time generally known by both the French and English.

SABBATH DAY POINT.

During the Revolution, it is *said,* a fight occurred here between some Militia and a party of Tories and Indians. The Americans gained the victory, the killed and wounded of the enemy numbering about forty. The view up the lake from this point is one of rare beauty. And look — Black Mountain is now

(1) — See Lossing's Field Book, Vol. i.

fully itself once more, lifting up its dark, but gracefully defined peak in sharp contrast with the deep blue sky, while all the surrounding parts of the landscape, which form the accessories of this mountain, sink into their true and subordinate positions. Throughout the entire central portion of the lake, Black Mountain seems to *travel* with the tourist, and presents itself in the midst of every new view. The student of nature will be amply repaid by watching its various aspects.

The point opposite Sabbath Day Point, is Bluff Point, beyond which, on the east shore, are the Odell Islands; while on the west, about the same distance, may be seen the Scotch Bonnet. Two miles to the north of the Bonnet, is the little village of Hague, where the steamer stops for passengers. Sailing on from Hague, we pass Cook's Island and then Friends' Point, where two scouting-parties belonging to the same force, once met, and in the darkness of the night came near firing upon one another. Two miles below Hague, on the east shore, will be seen Anthony's Nose, a bold and lofty hill, with rocks jutting out into the lake. There are three other places in the State that bear the name of the Old Saint, who, evidently, for some reason not so clear, was a great favorite. One is on the Hudson, forming the southern limit of the Highlands, and two others are situated on the Mohawk. At this point may be found the deepest water of the lake. A fisherman in his boat once narrowly escaped drowning in the huge waves caused by a rock that fell into the lake from Anthony's Nose. In the hill opposite, the guides used to point out a dozen mortars in a solid rock, which, they avered, were made by the Indians for the purpose of pounding corn.

Two miles farther down, on the west shore, is Rogers' Slide. This is a steep, smooth precipice of

ROGERS' SLIDE.

naked rock, inclining at a sharp angle, in the face of the mountain. It forms a prominent object from the lake, and, in 1757, was called "Bald Mountain," by Father Roubaud, in his Relation. At the foot of the Slide the water is quite deep. It received its present name, it is alleged, from the fact that Rogers the Ranger was once surprised here by the Indians, and made his escape on the ice. The latest version of the story runs somewhat as follows:

In the winter of 1758 Rogers was surprised by some Indians, while out on a scout, and put to flight.

Shod with snow-shoes, he eluded pursuit, and, coming to this spot, saved his life by an ingenious device. Descending the mountain, until he came to the edge of the precipice, he threw his haversack down upon the ice, unbuckled his snow-shoes, and, without moving them, turned himself about, and put them on his feet again, with the heels in front. He then retreated by the way he came, until he reached the southern brow of the rock, where he found a ravine, down which he escaped, and sped away on the ice towards Fort George. The Indians, in the meanwhile, came to the spot, and, seeing the double set of tracks, concluded that they were made by two persons who had thrown themselves down the cliff, rather than to fall into their hands. But, on looking about, they saw Rogers disappearing in the distance on the ice, and, believing that he slid down the cliff, concluded that he was under the special protection of the Great Spirit. They then gave up the chase.

So runs the latest version of the story. But, in 1802, the cliff was called Rogers' Rock, not Rogers' *Slide.* The best account Dwight could get at that time, was, that he escaped down a valley, and that the Indians supposed he fell off the precipice. Dwight's guide told him that one Colonel Cochrane and several others escaped in the same way, and that years after, when surveying the land, he showed his companions a bullet, fired at him on this occasion, lodged in a tree. The earliest account, however, simply says, that there was a *tradition* that a man once escaped from the savages in some such way. But what is worse, Rogers, who is very prolix where his own adventures are concerned, says nothing whatever about the affair in his journal; which most persons will accept as good proof that it never occurred.

Rogers was a New-Hampshire man, whose brutal character is illustrated by his deeds. After the French war he went to England, and while there dined in company with some officers, who agreed, over their wine, that the person who could tell the greatest falsehood should have his bill paid by the others. When Rogers' turn came, he told the company that his father was shot by a friend, who mistook him for a bear; that his mother was followed in the snow, on a stormy day, by a hunter, who supposed he was following the tracks of a panther: and that when a small boy, he travelled on foot in the woods, ten miles, with birch brooms on his shoulder, having nothing to guide him but marks on the trees. Judgment was at once uproariously given in his favor by the company.[1]

Rogers returned to America when the Revolution broke out, but was suspected by Washington as a spy, and could get no employment. He eventually obtained a commission from the English commander, and raised a company of Tory Rangers, which, on Long Island and elsewhere, proved more or less a scourge. He was proscribed by the New-Hampshire

(1)—New Hampshire Coll., Vol. i., p. 240.

Legislature, who decreed a divorce for his wife. Neither the time, place, nor the manner of his death is given.

But while thus dwelling upon the story of Rogers, we have been nearing the foot of the lake, whose waters, at this point, begin to shoal. It decreases in depth until the outlet is reached, where the water, now somewhat discolored by clay, passes through a narrow creek, and tumbles over the falls, on its way to Lake Champlain, making a descent of about two hundred and forty feet in the course of four miles. At this end of the lake there is nothing of special interest to detain the traveller, before proceeding to Ticonderoga; though he will, of course, notice the little island called Prisoners' Island, where, tradition says, the French sometimes confined their prisoners, and from which a party once escaped by wading across a shallow place to the main land, on the west shore.

The French called this island *Isle au Mouton*.[1] It probably made a convenient sheep-fold. Schuyler and Martin, who, in 1758, were returned by Abercrombie as Montcalm's prisoners on the expiration of their parole, were received on this island by the advanced guard of the French.

(1) — Col. Doc., Vol. x. p. 759.

THE LAKE IN THE SEASONS.

CHAPTER III.

O me, my pleasant rambles by the lake,
My sweet, mild, fresh three-quarters of a year,
My one Oasis in the dust and drouth
Of city life. — *Tennyson.*

Spring — Summer — Boating — Echoes — Progressive Change — Sunrise — Sunset — Autumn — Black Mountain — Jefferson — Indian Summer — Winter — Ice.

WHOEVER desires to know Lake George thoroughly, will find it necessary to study all its varied moods, which are as changeable as the sky. Yet it has certain general characteristics in each of the four seasons. The early spring is, perhaps, the least interesting season of the year. When the snow disappears, the ravages of winter become apparent. The woods everywhere have a black and sodden look. The oaks, which retain their dusky foliage much longer than the other trees, and part with their leaves as reluctantly as the belle loses her charms, are now completely stripped; and the woods, except where the evergreen pine appears, wear an aspect of extreme poverty and desolation. The action of the frost is revealed even on the rocks.

Eventually, the warm-breathing air of the south comes, and the vegetable kingdom feels the thrill of a new life. Imperceptibly, the tone of the landscape is changed, and the hills, and islands, and shores, are suffused with a pale, delicate emerald green. At this time, a day of genial, sunny weather causes a sudden growth of verdure that will transform the whole lake. Then the water, which previously had reflected the leafless trees and cheerless hills, is lighted up with beauty, and in the sunlight gleams with the richest hues. Joy and gladness then seem to fill the very air. At this period the showers on the lake are very fine.

But spring soon gives away to summer, which rapidly shoots up into its green prime, when the country is thronged with visitors from every part of the United States. Lake George at this time presents the most lovely picture. The majority of transient visitors congregate at Caldwell, and here, all day long, the water is covered with boats containing parties engaged in fishing, rowing, and in excursions to the islands. We need not go abroad on Italian lakes, or sail in Venetian gondolas, in order to witness picturesque scenes. Often on Lake George the boating parties, arrayed in bright costumes, reflected on the waves, with the accessories of green hills, blue skies, and sparkling water, form scenes that never fail to delight the artist's eye. There is no end of song and merry-making. Under the shadow of French Mountain, from the summit of which, in the spring of 1757, Rigaud reconnoitred Fort William Henry, will be found a remarkably good echo, which, in a calm day, will repeat with great fidelity all the variations of the bugle or flute. Visitors often row to this spot. It is easily found, and then

> . . . "Many a laugh and many a shout
> The busy echoes toss about,
> Till joyous with the merry rout
> The hills are pealing."

To describe a day of summer-time here, would be a difficult task. From dawn until evening the lake is the subject of progressive change, and is continually going on from glory to glory. Sunrise often presents a scene of rare beauty. In the course of the night the mist accumulates among the hills and on the surface of the lake, and the first act of Old Sol, is to drive it away. This is a gradual work. As a range of mountains extends along the east side of the lake, we first view the light in the sky overhead, which gleams with red and gold. But as the day advances, French Mountain doffs its nightcap, and the sunbeams, bursting through the tree-tops, charge down the declivities upon the fleecy fog, like angelic spears. Unable to withstand the assault, the misty battalions break and fly. In due time the work is thoroughly finished, and

"Now flaming up the heavens, the potent sun
Melts into limpid air the high-raised clouds
And morning fogs, that hovered round the hills
In parti-colored bands; till wide unveiled
The face of Nature shines, from where earth seems
Far-stretched around to meet the bending sphere."

As the day wears on, it is delightful to lounge around the lake, watching its changeful mood, as its surface is rippled by the wind, or shaded by some passing cloud. About noon the air will often be charged with a fine haze, which gives greater apparent depth and distance to the view. There is then a wide scope for the imagination, and, under its influence, the mountains seem to increase in height, presenting at the same time a softer outline. Everything in the distance is seen through a strongly refracted light, so that it is often difficult to tell where shore and water meet; while some of the little transfigured islands appear as if rising towards the sky. To the landscape painter, the lake at such times affords a rare study. A gentle breeze, however, is always sufficient to dispel these effects. Late in the afternoon, the sun swings around on the west side of the lake, when the hills gradually extend their shadows along its entire length, except at Bolton, ten miles down, where the range descends, and allows the King of Day to fling his beams with full force across the water upon the opposite mountains. The sunset is enjoyed to its fullest extent by the passengers who come up the lake at this hour from Ticonderoga; while the view, looking down from Caldwell, is much finer than in the morning. There lie the mountains towards the north, eight miles distant, vested in purple, each rock and crag a gleaming gem, while the roseate sky, barred with rich purple and green, is mirrored on the smooth lake, which, when ploughed by the homeward-bound Minnehaha, glitters like a sea of gold.

Erelong the sun sinks to rest, and the splendor fades, leaving only a deep purple glow, which gives way to a black pall. Before it is too late, however, the visitor must take a boat and row out into the middle of the lake, to observe the richness of the shadows on the water, and the color of the surrounding hills. Then all that is unsightly is obscured, and the rich green of field and wood becomes wonderfully softened, and yet intensified, in the gloaming light, which is now reflected wholly from above by the canopy of deep blue. At this time the reflection of the green hills gives the water a beauty that the artist strives in vain to convey, especially when it is marked by those trails of light that follow in the track of some belated boat or Indian canoe. But finally the twilight dies away, the mountains are reduced to dusky, indistinguishable forms, and the lake is left to the meek-eyed stars, which, here and there, sow a jewel in the wave.

But after all that can be said about summer, autumn is the most beautiful portion of the year, though few visitors linger to enjoy its glories. At this season,

Dame Nature, like an old coquette, puts on her most gorgeous robes, and strives to appear young. How magnificent the hues! The mountains appear all aflame with glory. Sunsets and rainbows appear to have fallen down upon them, and all their borders seem covered with rich Cashmere shawls.

There is a radical difference between the American and European autumn. Indeed, Tacitus speaks of some old Germans who knew nothing at all about it. Autumn in England and on the continent appears tame, while in America it is the true carnival time. The splendor of our autumn is to be accounted for by the fact that in America we have a far greater variety of forest trees. In France, for instance, there are only about forty species that grow to the height of thirty feet, while in America there are no less than one hundred and forty. Around Lake George there is the usual variety, so that the hills blaze, and yet, like the Burning Bush, are not consumed. Here and there may sometimes be found only a few varieties, and then, as Moir says of the English forests in autumn,

> "The faded woods a *yellow* livery wear."

The west side of Black Mountain appears from a distance to have only some maples and birches (the latter predominating) besides the pines; hence it is chiefly marked around its side with zones of green and yellow. But elsewhere there is no lack of color, the crimson and scarlet being of the deepest and most exquisite hue. Jefferson visited the lake in June, 1791, accompanied by Mr. Madison, while Washington was on a southern tour, and improved a part of his vacation in the use of his rod and gun, at the same time giving some attention to natural history, a science in which he excelled, and which, but for the claims of his country, would probably have occupied a much larger portion of his life. Writing about the botany of the lake, he said of the trees: "Those either unknown or rare in Virginia, were the sugar-maple, in great abundance; the silver fir, the white pine, pitch pine, spruce pine, a shrub with decumbent stems which they call juniper, an aralea, very different from the mundiflora, with very large clusters of flowers, more thickly set on branches, of a deeper red, and a high pink fragrance. It is the richest shrub I have seen. The honeysuckle of the gardens grows wild on the banks of Lake George; the paper birch, an aspen with a velvet leaf, a shrub willow with downy catkins, a wild gooseberry, and a wild cherry with a single fruit (not in the bunch cherry), and strawberries in abundance."[1]

These are some of the trees and shrubs not found in Virginia, but they form a small portion of the flora of the lake, which the philosopher admired quite as much as the magnificent pickerel and trout. And when the

(1)—Jefferson's Works, Vol. iii. p. 265.

leaves ripen,[1] the forests display every conceivable color. It is then a rare pleasure to watch the reflections of the mountains on the water. Of course, the weather will not always serve our purpose. Cold, disagreeable days come, when we are fitly reminded of the words of Ossian: "Arise, winds of autumn, arise: blow along the heath! streams of the mountain, roar! roar, tempests, in the grove of my oaks!"

Still, there are not wanting beautiful days when the sky and air are in harmony with the resplendent hues of the forest, and when the lake appears like some sweet scene of enchantment. Then the little rich, russet-colored isles, nestling in the shining lake, look like apples of gold in pictures of silver, while the tall, maple-crowned hill, looming up in the distance, seems a pyramid of fire. Whoever takes two or three of these glorious days for a trip down the lake, will store up in the portfolio of his mind a succession of beautiful scenes that will last for life.

And when autumn declines, and the magnificent foliage has disappeared, then comes the Indian Summer; though many persons unacquainted with its characteristics place it earlier in the season. It usually occurs about All Saints' Day, November 1st, and by some of the French who visited the lake it was known as the Summer of All Saints. On the continent of Europe it is called the Summer-Close, and in Eng-

(1) — The frost has nothing to do with changing the color of the leaves in autumn.

land, Martin-mass Summer, as the peasantry look for it about St. Martin's Day, which falls on November 11th. This season is marked by a reddish, hazy, quiet atmosphere, and a slight rise in the temperature. In the autumn the haze is not always seen around the lake. After the September and October rains the sky is sometimes attended by a wondrous clearness and depth. We may always measure the purity of the air by the clearness of the reflections in the water. When the air is perfectly free from mist, the maple torch flames as brightly in the water of the lake at your feet as on the rocky cliff above your head. But during the Indian Summer, the lake is always veiled in mist. Longfellow happily describes it in Evangeline:

"Such was the advent of autumn. Then followed that beautiful season
Called by the pious Acadian peasants, the Summer of All Saints.
Filled was the air with a dreamy and magical light; and the landscape
Lay as if created in all the freshness of childhood.
Peace seemed to reign upon earth, and the restless heart of the ocean
Was for a moment consoled. All sounds were in harmony blended.
Voices of children at play, the crowing of cocks in the barn-yards,
Whir of wings in the drowsy air, and the cooing of pigeons,
All were subdued and low as the murmurs of love, and the great sun
Looked with the eye of love through the golden vapors around him."

Many persons suppose that the Indian Summer is distinguished only by a rise in the temperature; and when, as is sometimes the case, Old Sol falls back into one of his July dreams, they tell us that the Indian Summer has come. But we must observe more carefully, as the season brings no obtrusive phenomena. We hailed it once on Lake George, near Sabbath

Day Point. For several days the weather had been unpropitious, but at last there came a day when earth seemed caught up into heaven. Then the landscape was bathed in a warm, rich haze, and mountain and valley, and field and upland, still crimsoned with a few autumnal tints, shone with a subdued but royal splendor. The lake was covered with a fine veil of mist, while overhead, the sky was as blue as sapphire. The insects, invigorated by the genial warmth, had come forth to add another hour to their brief day of life, and were gaily chirping among the branches, or skimming along the calm surface of the lake, unmindful of the morrow's frost. Occasionally on the shore could be heard the voice of a trudging farmer driving the patient ox; but these were all the sounds that broke the stillness. Black Mountain towered above the lake, having an almost supernatural aspect, while the whole landscape appeared invested with a vague, dreamy life, so that there was an almost irresistible temptation to accept the transcendental definition of the universe as "a projection of God in the unconscious." It was the Indian Summer. And days like these are few and brief; yet if they vanish like a beautiful dream, they give us a lovely night. As Whittier writes:

"From gold to gray,
Our mild sweet day
Of Indian Summer fades too soon;
But tenderly,
O'er lake and lea,
Hangs, white and calm, the Hunter's Moon."

Winter is a northern word that was first used to denote the period of windy weather. It now stands for different things in different latitudes. How unlike is winter at the equator and the poles. In one case it is the season of night and frost, and in the other, of sunshine and flowers, and eternal spring. In some regions, lying within the torrid zone, winter surpasses all other portions of the year in loveliness. There the traveller fails to witness the grand march of the seasons; there he sees no changeful autumn and no general decay. Nature undergoes an imperceptible renovation, and is always in her green prime, though, at certain seasons of the year, the heat increases, and the leaves seem to droop. At such times the air is often stifling, and the entire animal creation feels a sense of oppression. Erelong, however, the clouds gather, the blinding flash comes, followed by the thunder's peal, and then the sky sends down the welcome rain. But soon the tempest dies away, and the sun looks out upon the reviving earth and smiles. And this is winter. Here in the tropics

> "The seasons alter: hoary-headed frosts
> Fall in the fresh lap of the crimson rose,
> And on Old Hiem's thin and icy crown
> An odorous chaplet of sweet summer buds
> Is as in mockery set."

But at Lake George, as the reader may surmise, the seasons follow in their appointed course. Early in November the trees are nearly laid bare, while fleets of crisped leaves, rich and varied in their hues, are launched by the wind upon the shimmering lake, where they voyage for a brief time like mimic argosies and gay gondolas, and then sink to the bottom with Montcalm's boats and Abercrombie's batteaux. Then the farmers bring home from the field the remains of their crops, and prepare for the cold weather, which is a season of isolation; while the boys improve the occasion to lay in their stores of nuts, and beat about the woods with their guns in search of game. About Christmas the lake is frozen over, and by New Year's day its surface is transformed into a solid marble highway. In the meanwhile the snow has fallen, and the mountains — vested in October with such magnificent robes — are sheeted in white from base to summit. The sleigh-bells resound along the roads and on the lake, a slippery course where all may enter free. The wood-cutter improves this season to get wood and timber from the islands, which the sharply-shod oxen draw home on sleds. In the sheltered coves the skater enjoys his sport without fear, as the intense cold which prevails in this season gives a great thickness of ice. It is a merry season. Go forth upon the banks of the lake, and you will hear the joyous shout and see the blazing bonfire. As Percival says:

"Below me rings the lake,
The stars above me burn;
Away the skaters break,
And glide, and wheel, and turn."

The water at this time rises nearly two feet above the summer level, which fact is duly registered upon the rocks.

In March the ice begins to soften and break up, but it does not dissolve so rapidly as on Lake Champlain, where its sudden disappearance leads some of the farmer-folk to imagine that it sinks to the bottom. Before the ice parts, and indeed at intervals during the whole winter, it gives out loud reports. This, however, is not peculiar to Lake George. Southey speaks of it in his journal, under date of Feb. 1, 1814. He says the noise was "neither like thunder nor the sound of wind, but a long, moaning, melancholy sound, rising and dying away, beyond measure mournful." He adds, as we can well believe, that to any one crossing the ice, "it is inexpressibly awful and appalling." So Wordsworth writes:

> "From under Esthwaite's splitting fields of ice
> The pent-up air, struggling to free itself,
> Gave out to meadow, ground, and hill, a loud
> Protracted yelling, like the noise of wolves
> Howling in troops along the Bothnia main."

This resemblance to the howling of wolves has been noticed by others. Southey, in his journal above quoted, says that his children suggested the idea when they heard it. Whoever would judge for himself must not be content with a brief summer trip to the lake, but must live here all the year round. The artist, at least, might possibly conclude about Lake George as Philip Hamerton did of Loch Awe:

"I passed Loch Awe as tourists do,
Catching glimpses here and there,
Of the scenes we posted through;

With companions full of care
About the comforts of the inns,
And about to-morrow's fare.

Thus the soul, to try it, wins
Glimpses of its Paradise.
'Twas a judgment for my sins:

Yet a judgment making wise,
For I went another year
To work alone, and settled there."

AMONG THE ISLANDS.

CHAPTER IV.

> To burst all link of habit — then to wander far away,
> On from island unto island, at the gateways of the day.
>
> —*Tennyson.*

ATLANTIS — ST. BRANDON — LOCH AWE — LAKE GEORGE — EXPLORING — SCOUTING — RECLUSE — DOME ISLAND — CAMPING OUT — TENNYSON'S "ISLET" — EXPLORING — MIRAGE — BOATING — VIRGIL — LOCH KATRINE — SHELVING ROCK FALL.

HE subject of islands has possessed a peculiar charm in all ages of the world. It was on an island that the ancients located the abode of happy departed spirits. Their dreams of that favored place were colored by the rose. The Odyssey, describing the fabled Atlantis, says: "There the life of mortals must be easy; there is no snow, nor winter, nor much rain, but ocean is ever sending up the shrilly-breathing zephyrus to refresh man." In those days islands were not always stationary. Delos, celebrated as the birthplace of Apollo, once floated under the sea. And later, St. Brandon was a flying island, which gyrated somewhere west of the Canaries. It figured in all the maps at the time of Columbus, and was retained on a French chart in 1755. This imaginary island was named after a Scotch abbot of the sixth century, who undertook to find the *Islands* of *Paradise.* Several expeditions went in search of the Abbot's isle, one party sailing from Spain in 1721. It was generally believed to be the retreat of their lost King Roderigo. There, also, was located the garden of Armida, where Rinaldo remained enchanted.

But we can readily excuse the enchantment. Rinaldo would have been enchanted almost anywhere among the islands of Lake George, which are unsurpassed for beauty. They vary in size, some being no larger than that island of Shakspeare, which the jesting sailor consigned to the Duke's pocket, while others cover a considerable extent. Occasionally they afford standing-room for no more than a single tree, though at other times supporting a good sized forest. They occur singly, in pairs, and in groups, and are scattered all through the lake. At the Narrows they nearly block up the passage. But how shall we account for the islands?

The peasants around Loch Awe, as we are told by Philip Hamerton,[1] held that the islands in that lake

(1)—See Isles of Loch Awe.

were the crests of pastoral hills which rose in Arcadian valleys ages long ago. One Bera, a coarse Diana, owned the vale, and it was her nightly duty to cover a spring, in the neighboring mountain, with a huge stone. This precaution being neglected, it would result in the overflow of the spring and the inundation of the valley. But on one occasion Bera left the spring uncovered. The next morning, to her utter dismay, a fearful cataract burst forth and submerged the valley, leaving the lesser hills with their tops just above the flood. And

> "So was the peaceful valley of the Awe
> Flooded and drowned forever. Ask no more."

This tradition tells us of a geological fact, and equally indicates the origin of the Isles of both Lake George and Loch Awe. Where our lake now lies was once an empty valley, barred with low hills built of the primitive rock, with which the valley is floored. When the rain period set in — ages long ago — the streams ran down the sides of the naked hills and filled up the valley. At first the islands were

> . . . . . "Barren rocks
> Glittering with white quartz crystals here and there,
> Scattered like spots of snow upon the hills;"

but, eventually, what the geologist calls the "drift" period dawned, and a mighty deluge then swept over the whole country, rising above the tops of the highest mountains, and covering hill and valley with deposits of loose earth, gravel, and sand. When the flood passed away, and the lake was drained down to its former level, the islands emerged again, though the most of them were now covered with a deep soil, from which sprang the green groves of beech, and oak, and pine. But for the barrier at the lower end of the lake, the space it occupies would have become a rich, populated valley. But now we see

> "The town unbuilt, the mountain barriers closed,
> And all the concave valley with its park,
> Embattled hall, and avenues of oak,
> And hundred farms, a sheet of silent water."

On the whole, however, no one is a loser. Lakes like Lake George have frequently been called the eyes of the landscape; and surely the utilitarian could not have the heart to put them out.

The work of exploring the islands is one that might well occupy the most of an ordinary vacation, though it is not a work that would compensate the class of persons who incline to lounge away the summer on the piazza of the hotel. Good views may be had from his easy-going carriage, even by the invalid, but to see and know the islands thoroughly, we must use a pair of oars. For the most part they remain substantially as they were two hundred years ago, and it is not a difficult task for the tourist, with the records of the olden times before him, to "conjure up again the evanished shapes . . ; people these isles, this rock; and cause, by might of spirit and power, the

FOURTEEN-MILE ISLAND.

old times to flit by, clearly and truly." He will thus live over the past in the society of Father Roubaud, Chevalier St. Ours, Montcalm, Rogers, Putnam, and scores of other brave and adventurous spirits.

Between the years 1755 and 1760, scouting among the islands was almost a distinct branch of the military profession, and the "Rangers," as they were called, proceeded from point to point, in small parties, camping and fighting as they went. The traces of their stockades and camps have in most cases passed away, yet we can row from isle to isle, and follow them in their adventures with the utmost certainty.

From the pivotal positions afforded by the islands, we may obtain the best views of the scenery. On the north shore of Recluse Island, the view is had in its perfection. Tongue Mountain rises a little to the left; directly in front, the Narrows partially unbar their beautiful gates; Shelving Rock and Dome Island—the latter rejoicing in its green crown—lift themselves on the right; while Black Mountain looms grandly in the distance. Nothing could be more exquisite than the view which is here enjoyed, and the proprietor of the island has shown the most excellent taste in building his summer cottage on this romantic spot.

Dome Island, mentioned above with Green Island, stands higher above the water than all the rest. The latter is heavily wooded with beech, birch, hemlock, pine, and other trees, and offers a splendid site for a summer home, where, through the loop-holes in the dense wood, the eye is delighted with the ever-changing beauty of the lake. Yet in the centre of the island it would be easy for one to imagine himself in the heart of some forest thousands of miles away; and the lover of solitude is as secluded and free from intrusion as Cicero, when meditating among the wild old woods of the Island of Astura, on the shore of the Tyrrhenian Sea.

On any of the islands in the central parts of the lake, the fisherman or the artist will find most excel-

UNDER CANVASS.

lent spots to pitch his summer tent. If the weather should not always prove propitious, it will at least appear that

> "A summer night in greenwood spent,
> Were but to-morrow's merriment."

Even in a pelting storm the woodsman will find a safe

covert, and from his seat at the cosy camp-fire he can look out on the misty lake, blistered by the rain, with entire unconcern. The islands here are quite unlike that pictured by Tennyson, in his poem of the "Islet." The little singer's wife could not say:

> "For in all that exquisite isle, my dear,
> There is but one bird with a musical throat,
> And his compass is but of a single note,
> That it makes me weary to hear."

It is the charm of the islands that there is no monotony. The lake is a kaleidoscope that is never at rest. It speaks eloquently of mutation in both sunshine and storm; and here it is easy to believe, with the Ettrick Shepherd, that there is no such thing as bad weather. Whoever, therefore, wishes to enjoy himself to the utmost, should take to his oars, and go forth a sort of Vasco de Gama upon this island sea, and explore the islands in their order, taking from each, as he passes, a tithe of arrow or spear-heads as souvenirs of the voyage. He will find, as he goes on, that nearly every island is a lifting up of the lake's floor, which slopes away from the rock-strewn strand into the clear sunlit depths below, the home of the bass and pike. Sometimes, when a *mirage* invests the lake, they seem to mock approach; and on a windy day, when the waves break on the rocks, they are liable to knock a hole in the bottom of your boat; but, plumed as they are with green trees, they usually wave a welcome from afar, and invite the weary to repose under the shade of wide-spread natural tents.

Nothing could be more charming than to idle for a day on Lake George. For this purpose, a sail-boat is not always desirable. The breeze is sometimes too fickle to be trusted. The dead calm is often followed by the fitful gust or heavy squall, which rushes down from hill-side and mountain. On the whole it is better for those unused to sails to depend upon oars, since while these last, a good boat is safe in any weather. Whoever takes the time to row around the lake will feel amply rewarded. Whenever he tires of the oar, numberless sweet retreats will invite him to rest. If a brief summer shower overtakes him, he can find temporary protection under the shaggy pines and jutting cliffs; and when the sun looks out, he may, at times, view the most magnificent rainbows spanning the lake from shore to shore. If weary of gazing, the fishing-rod awaits the disciple of Izaak Walton, who will soon find that the lake keeps some of its sweetest thoughts "expressed in trout." If his strength fails, the passing steamer will take him on board, and tow his boat home. And if he *should* find himself belated some night, he will have no cause to complain of the moonlight or the stars; while every farm-house on the shore will prove as hospitable as a hotel.

In voyaging amid these beautiful islands, one familiar with the early records will wonder that the scenery made so little impression upon those who traversed the lake. The loveliness of the scenery is never alluded to, and from such accounts as those of

Father Roubaud, it would be easy to conclude that the writer was sailing on a common pond. The men of those days were completely absorbed in thoughts of war and trade, and from their pens Lake St. Sacrament does not gain the poorest tribute. And yet writers like Bancroft now often pause in the midst of grave, historical narrations, to portray, here and there, some charming scene which has riveted their attention and caused an exclamation of surprise. How beautifully does he speak of the crystal waves, the breezy isles, and the mountains stepping down to the shores. He says, "Peacefully rest the waters of Lake George between their rampart of highlands. In their pellucid depths, the cliffs, and the hills, and the trees trace their image, and the beautiful region speaks to the heart, teaching affection for nature."[1] And yet this "affection for nature," as we have already remarked, was something rare in early times. There seems to be a period in the history of all nations, when the finest exhibitions of nature have no power to excite admiration. We find that the lovely lakes of England, Ireland and Scotland, were wholly unappreciated by the best of the old writers. Even the early English poets are dumb on the subject of Windermere, Loch Awe, and Killarney. During the fifteenth, sixteenth, and seventeenth centuries, those beautiful regions were well known, but they had no message for the most culti-

(1)—Hist., Vol. iv. p. 259.

vated minds. It was so with the Italian Lakes even in the Augustan Age. Virgil, who was born near the shores of Como, only says:

> "Our spacious lakes; thee, Larius [Como]; and next
> Bernacus, with tempestuous billows vex't."[1]

And yet the lakes have no lack of admirers *now;* while at Lake George the tide of travel is increasing every year. Men of taste who have frittered away much time at the hackneyed watering-places scattered throughout the country, often feel like the author of the following lines, who says,

> "O timid heart! with thy glad throbs
> Some self-reproach is blended,
> At the long years that died before,
> The sight of scene so splendid."

One does not know, when on the lake, what feature to admire most. It is a feast of beauty all the way through. Willis declares that in this respect, as well as others, it excels Loch Katrine. Speaking on this point he says, "Loch Katrine at the Trosachs, is a miniature likeness of Lake George. It is the only lake in Europe that has at all the same style and degree of beauty. . . . Loch Katrine can scarcely be called picturesque, except at the Trosachs, while Lake George throughout all the mazes of its . . islands, preserves the same wild . . character of beauty." Indeed, one always feels that the *last* view is the *best.*

(1) — Georg. ii., l. 159.

We have spoken of camping out on the islands, but this mode of life is not imperative. On Fourteen Mile Island, opposite Bolton, is a good hotel, surrounded by many attractions. Near by is the sweetest waterfall to be found around the lake. It is easily reached in boating. Shelving Rock Fall is situated on a small stream which empties into Shelving Rock Bay, about a mile south of Fourteen Mile Island. It is found a few rods from the beach, and all its accessories have been arranged by nature with admirable artistic effect. Shelving Rock Fall is not a Niagara, even in miniature,—and in the White Mountain region, where numberless cascades leap down the hill-sides, and bound from crag to crag, our little fall would be passed without notice; yet it is a perfect gem, and at Lake George, where cascades are not numerous, it is fully appreciated. Silently flowing out from its covert of dark green foliage, the stream glides along its stony bed until it meets a large boulder, when it divides into two parts and springs foaming down the declivity, uniting again before reaching its basin below, from whence it flows, singing and shimmering towards the tranquil lake. This is one of the most charming spots on the lake for a picnic, and well repays the tourist for the time spent on a trip among the islands.

IN GENERAL.

CHAPTER V.

The Old Man of the Fort — Rattlesnakes — Relics — Jacques Courtois — Lake Deposits — An Old Vessel — Indian Graves — A Nepistingue Burial — Fish — Fishing — Shooting — Squirrels — Geology — Gems.

ANTIQUITIES in general is a subject that must not be omitted in the account of Lake George, especially at the present time, when there is a revived interest in everything ancient, and when so many individuals are glad to enter upon "the constant service of the antique world." This department is interesting, if not very extensive, and has always engaged the attention of some one of the odd characters that haunt the lake.

About the year 1830, there was a person of this sort at Caldwell. He was known by visitors as "The Old Man of the Fort," and his name sometimes made its way into the metropolitan papers. He came originally from Massachusetts, and had known the lake during forty-five of his seventy-six years of existence. "Old Dick," as he was often called, knew just where to find the rattlesnakes, which were very plentiful on Cobble Hill and Black Mountain, though they are rare enough now. He carried on quite a thriving trade in rattlesnakes, and used to practice the difficult art of extracting their fangs. He often travelled up and down the lake on the steamboat, where he kept a box of snakes for exhibition. On his box was the following inscription: "In this box ar a Rattell Snaick Hoo was Kecht on Blak Mounting. He is seven years old last Guly. Admittance sixpents site, children half price or nothen." The latter clause he thought extremely witty.

The Old Man of the Fort has left no successor, yet there are several persons known as rattlesnake hunters; one of whom usually gets up quite a little stock of antiquities every year to dispose of to the summer visitors. There is but very little doubt about the genuine character of these specimens. A diligent search would result in the discovery of many objects of interest. The grounds around the village of Caldwell are full of mementos of the past. Scarcely a foot of soil can be upturned without bringing to light some relic of the French and English wars. In excavating for cellars, the laborer's spade uncovers the grave of both soldier and savage, who often found promiscuous sepulture. Around Fort George may be dug up fragments of bombshell, together with a variety of souvenirs of a similar character, collections of which may be seen in the museums of the hotels. The site of what is called the Old French Burying-Ground is still pointed out near the foot of Rattlesnake Cobble. The ground has frequently been examined by those interested in the antiquities of the lake, and the owner was finally obliged to prohibit investigations. At one time there was a stone standing on this spot inscribed, "Jacques Courtois, 1755."[1] A brief biography, indeed. It indicates that he lived and died. He was, perhaps, attached to Dieskau's army in some capacity, and came from sunny France to America with many high anticipations. Wealth, honor, and renown, all floated before his eyes, but he found, like multitudes of his countrymen, only a bloody grave.

There are numberless treasures in the lake, where they are at present likely to remain. During the French war and the war of the Revolution, hundreds of boats, batteaux, and small craft, were destroyed in a single day. Some were burned and others sunk. Many vessels, loaded with war material, went down in deep water, where the diver would to-day find whole batteries of rusty cannon, and muskets without number. Within a recent period the fisherman has seen here and there, at the bottom of the lake, bat-

(1)—April 11, 1754, six French deserters came to Albany from Niagara, by the way of Oswego. Among them was "Jean Baptiste de Cortois" (French Comte). It is *possible* that this is the same person. The French deserters often enlisted in English regiments. Col. Doc. vi. p. 832.

teaux, apparently filled with barrels, while others say they have seen cannon. Artillery, shot, and shell were frequently secreted in the lake, as well as on the land, by both the French and English, and much of this material remains where it was deposited. Abercrombie sunk a large vessel of one hundred tons, near Fort William Henry, to keep her from falling into the hands of the enemy. This vessel was afterwards raised, and employed by Lord Amherst in 1759. The hull of a large vessel is still seen in fair, calm weather, and appears to be nearly full of cobble-stones, probably ballast. There the old craft has lain for an entire century,

> "Docked in the sand
> Vailing her high top lower than her ribs
> To kiss her burial."

The spot where this hulk may be seen is near the steamboat-landing, and can be found only when the lake is perfectly calm and the sky clear. Many years ago one of the residents of Caldwell undertook to raise the interesting relic, but failed, being able to get up only a portion of the timber of the bows. It is impossible to say what vessel this was, or whether it was built by the French or English. Perhaps it is the remains of the "Halifax," a vessel that Lord Amherst took with him in his expedition against Ticonderoga, in 1759. It is not too late to save what is still left, yet the keel of this old craft will never plough the lake again. Near Hague, on the shore of the lake, may be seen the remains of the steamer John Jay, which was destroyed by fire. On this occasion several lives were lost.

Around the lake may be found numerous relics of the Indians, such as stone knives, hatchets, and arrow-heads. On Recluse Island a number of the latter have been picked up, together with fragments of the material from which they are made, which shows that the place was once the site of an Indian dwelling, and that

> "There the ancient arrow-maker
> Made his arrow-heads of sandstone —
> Arrow-heads of chalcedony —
> Arrow-heads of flint and jasper,
> Smoothed and sharpened at the edges,
> Hard and polished, keen and costly."

Indian graves, except near battle-grounds, are not often found, though here and there on the hill-sides bordering the lake, and on the islands, may be seen what visitors sometimes imagine to be mounds, denoting places of sepulture. These are formed by the upturning of trees during the winter gales. Cart-loads of earth frequently adhere to the roots of large trees, and when they fall, it assumes the oblong shape of graves. In course of time the trunk of the tree decays, and nature neatly turfs over the mound, which has every appearance of being the work of man.[1] These

(1) — In the summer of last year (1867), the author saw a party of antiquarians opening one of these mounds. A large stone lay at each end, fully persuading them that the mound covered an Indian grave. Of course nothing was found.

mounds may be found in all stages of progress among the islands of the lake. Nevertheless, genuine Indian graves still exist. There must be one somewhere on the shore of the lake, near Montcalm's Bay, which the antiquary would deem a rare prize. It is the grave of a warrior who was killed in a fight at that place in 1757, on the evening before Montcalm arrived in front of Fort William Henry. The account of the burial is given by Father Roubaud, missionary of the Abenakis. He says:

"The morning had scarcely begun to dawn, when a party of the Nepistingue tribe proceeded with the funeral rites of their brother, killed during the action of the preceding night, and who died in the errors of paganism. His obsequies were celebrated with all pomp and savage splendor. The dead body had been arrayed in all its ornaments, or rather overloaded with all the trinkets that the most unusual degree of pride would be able to employ, under circumstances so sad in themselves. Collars of porcelain, silver bracelets, pendants for the ears and nose, magnificent dresses, all had been lavished on him. They had even called in the aid of paint and vermilion, to cover up under these brilliant colors, the pallid hue of death, and to give to his countenance an air of life, which in reality it did not possess. They had not been forgetful of any of the decorations of an Indian warrior. A gorget or neck-piece, bound with red ribbon, hung negligently on his breast; his gun resting on his arm, the tomahawk at his belt, the pipe in his mouth, the lance in his hand, and the kettle filled with provisions at his side. Clothed in this warlike and animated array, they had seated him on an eminence covered with grass, which served him for a bed of state."[1]

With a large number of those persons visiting the lake, everything relating to the fish will be of interest. It is very clear that the fish are not so abundant as formerly. The principal kinds taken are the bass, the pickerel, the perch, and the trout. Of the Lake George trout, Silliman says: "Nothing of the kind can be finer; this beautiful fish, elegantly decorated, and gracefully formed, shy of observation, and delighting, above all, in the perfect purity of its element, finds in Lake George a residence most happily adapted to its nature. Here it attains a very uncommon size, and exhibits its most perfect beauty and symmetry. The delicate carnation of its flesh, is here, also, most remarkable."[2]

His praise of the trout is certainly deserved. Trout are taken both in the lake and in the tributary brooks. The best fishing is found at the Narrows and in the vicinity of Cook's Island and Anthony's Nose. Trout Pavilion on the east side of the lake, about six miles from Caldwell, as well as Hague, are localities resorted to by lovers of fine fish.

(1)—Kip's Early Jesuits, p. 162.
(2)—Silliman's Tour, Vol. i. p. 152.

LANDING IN A SHOWER.

The fishermen must remember, however, that the fish of the lake are protected by special legislation. The law of 1812 prohibited the use of either seine or spear in taking fish in the lake or its tributaries. The law of 1824 was still more stringent, prohibiting angling, also, between September 1 and December 15. The law of 1853 stands as follows, though the amendment of 1855 makes an exception as regards those small fish which are taken for bait:

"It shall not be lawful for any person or persons to draw any seine, set any net, or spear any fish, in the waters of Lake George, or at or in the outlets or mouths of any brook, or creek entering into the same, at any season of the year; or to use any means or devices, angling excepted, to take or procure any fish in or from the waters of said lake, brooks, or creeks, at any season of the year; or to take any bass in said waters, or any of them between the first days of April and July in any year, in any manner, or by or under any device or pretence whatever."[1]

The hunter will not find himself without employment at the lake. During the fall and winter he may find an abundance of deer in the vicinity of Tongue Mountain. They are often driven into the lake and captured. In the right season there is always work to be done on land, with such members of the feathered tribe as the woodcock, the partridge, and the quail,

(1)—Rev. Stat., Chap. 506.

while on the lake he can watch his opportunity for a shot at the wild ducks. Besides the game-birds, the naturalist will find no small variety, and may bag excellent specimens of the gull, which always appears lonesome here on the lake; also the hawk, the loon, and, at times, the king of birds, the eagle.

At this place, whoever may be on the watch, will sometimes have an opportunity of seeing the squirrels travel, exaggerated accounts of whose performances on the water frequently get into popular works on natural history. On such occasions they go in search of food. A writer who hunted at the lake, at a somewhat recent period, gives the following account. He says:

"In the month of September, 1851, I arrived at Lake George, where I found that the gray and black squirrels had been travelling for several days, and were still moving. Early one morning I discovered three or four at several distances, swimming from the western to the eastern shore of the lake, which at that time was as smooth as glass. I watched them as long as I could see the ripples the water made, and supposed that they succeeded in crossing the lake, which at this point was more than a mile wide. . . . . I found many of both black and grey squirrels floating or lying along the shore of the lake, drowned. Persons frequently went after them in boats, and on putting down the oar before them, they would run up into the boat almost exhausted, where they were secured alive. I saw several that had been so taken at Lake George."[1]

The geologist will find abundant opportunities for study at Lake George, while the mineralogist can reap quite a harvest. The crystals of Diamond Island have already been spoken of in another place. At Rogers Slide may be found handsome garnets, resinite, coccolite, pyroxene, sphene, calcareous spar, and graphite; and, near by, tourmaline. The discovery of the latter mineral, in its amorphous condition, when it resembles anthracite, once caused some of the residents in the vicinity of the lake to believe that they had found a valuable bed of coal. A slight knowledge of geology would have taught them the impossibility of finding coal in primary rock; yet this discovery, led to a dispute, and ended in some unprofitable litigation.

Hematite occurs in the primitive rock at Anthony's Nose, which reddens with it in spots. Feldspar, epidote, and graphite also occur in Ticonderoga.

The sands of Lake George are particularly fine, and have a large interest apart from the beauty which they frequently give to the beach. Sand is the dust of the ages — the powdered foundation of the elder world. When obtained in its purest state it is composed of simple silex. But on the shores of the lake it is mixed with other materials. On the beach at Caldwell, a loadstone thrust into the sand will sometimes

(1) — DeVoe's Market Assistant, p. 123.

be drawn forth, covered, more or less, with a fine, glossy, black, magnetic iron-sand. There is also to be found limpid quartz, powdered garnet, and epidote. When mixed together, spread out loosely on a white paper, and viewed with a magnifying glass, they appear to very good advantage, and then if the lens should happen to be of great power, one might imagine that he had found a prize. Speaking of this sand, Silliman says: "It is indeed somewhat difficult to believe, that the garnet, and epidote, and probably coccolite, often rich in their colors, and highly translucent, are not ruby and chrysoberyl. It would be worth while," he adds, "to examine these sands more particularly, to ascertain if there may not be *gems* among them, as the gems of Ceylon and Brazil, and the hyacinths of Expaily in France are found among the alluvial ruin. . . . All similar sands should be examined with an attentive eye."[1]

A pinch of sand which the author once took home from Sabbath Day Point, and examined under an achromatic microscope of high power, afforded a rare exhibition. When brought into focus, and illuminated by the aid of a condenser, the effect was magical. A turn of the milled screw, and—*presto!*—the dull and, to the naked eye, almost colorless dust becomes an outspread heap of sparkling gems. One would think that he had suddenly come into the cave of some

(1)—Silliman's Tour, Vol. i. p. 172.

genii, so great is the profusion of epidote, garnet, amethyst, and crystal quartz. The rich colors of these minute fragments combine to form a beautiful exhibition, though one cannot help regretting the destruction of rich minerals involved in its production.

But the reader must not be kept longer from the consideration of the romantic history of Lake George.

COLONIAL DAYS.

> But see, the haughty household troops advance!
> The dread of Europe and the pride of France.

CHAPTER VI.

Champlain — Jogues — Courcelles — Nicholson's Expedition — The Battle of Lake George — Bloody Pond — The Retreat — Fort William Henry — Scouting — Loudon — Rigaud's Expedition — Father Roubaud — Montcalm — The Massacre.

THE existence of Lake George was first made known to Europeans by the French. In July, 1609, Champlain ascended the St. Lawrence, in company with a party of Hurons and Algonquins, and sailed across the lake which now bears his name. He had joined these Indians in an expedition against the hostile Iroquois, for the purpose of gaining their good will. As they proceeded on the way, the Indians described the country to be traversed, and the region which was inhabited by their enemies. Champlain says, "The Indians told me . . . that we must pass by a waterfall, *which I afterwards saw,*[1] and then enter another lake three or four leagues long." That lake was Lake George, the outlet of which, at Ticonderoga, forms a beautiful fall. This bold explorer never saw the lake itself.[2] Encountering their enemies near Crown Point, whither they had come to meet them, the Hurons and their confederates gained an easy victory by means of the arquebus of Champlain, and returned with ten or twelve prisoners.

The first white man who is known to have seen Lake George was Father Jogues.[3] May 29, 1646, he was on his way to the Mohawk country, to perfect a treaty. Attended by Jean Bourdon, the engineer, who was one of the principal residents of Quebec, he arrived in a canoe at the outlet of the lake on the eve of the festival of *Corpus Christi*,[4] and named it *Lac du St. Sacrement*,[5] Lake of the Blessed Sacrament. By

(1) — Doc. His. N. Y., Vol. iii. p. 5.

(2) — Charlevoix has been quoted by various authors, as saying that Champlain passed the rapids and sailed up Lake St. Sacrament; yet Charlevoix says nothing of the kind. His account of the matter indicates precisely the *contrary*.

(3) — Isaac Jogues, a member of the Society of Jesus, was born in Orleans, France, in 1607, and fell a martyr to the Faith in 1646, being cruelly murdered by the Mohawks, among whom he was laboring as a missionary. He was the first Roman Catholic missionary to enter the State of New York. When he left Canada to go on his mission, he had a presentiment of his coming fate, saying, *Ibo, nec redibo.*

(4) — A festival kept on the Thursday following Trinity Sunday, in commemoration of the supposed Real Presence of Christ in the Sacrament.

(5) — In giving it this name, the reference was *not* to the purity of the water. It was wholly in honor of the festival. See *Relations des Jesuites*, 1646, p. 15.

the Iroquois it had been known as Andiartarocte,[1] which meant the Tail of the Lake, i. e. the place where Lake Champlain closes. The next day they continued their course southward, on foot, "with great fatigue, for they had to carry on their backs their bundles and baggage." The Algonquin guides were forced to leave a great portion of their baggage on the border of the lake.

They reached their destination, accomplished their object, and June 16 started on their return. The Relation says: "They travelled several days by land, not without trouble, for they had, like Arabian horses, to carry their victuals and baggage, the brooks being the only taverns to be met with. Arriving on the border of Lake St. Sacrament, they made canoes, or small boats, with bark; and setting out in them, they paddled and sailed until the twenty-seventh of the same month of June, and then landed at the first French habitation."[2]

(1) — Father Bruyas in his MS. work on Mohawk *Radicals*, says: "*Ganniatare*, a lake: *Ganniatariakte*, I pass it with something." Potier, in his Huron Grammar, mentions *un* and *nd* as convertible. Hence the form *Gandiiatare*. Garocte means, "Go quickly." The name "Horikan" — Silvery Water — has no authority, and is simply a fancy of Cooper's.

(2) — Relation 1646, p. 18. Father Jogues has been represented (see Brodhead's New York, p. 423) as returning by the "same route" that he came. The authority given is Father Tanner's curious Latin work, compiled chiefly from the Relations. On this point he is clearly wrong, as well as in regard to the date of Father Jogues' return, which was on the 17th, and *not* the 16th, of June.

Father Jogues, therefore, was probably the first European who sailed upon the waters of the beautiful Lake of the Holy Sacrament.

It is true that others of the Fathers travelled in the vicinity about this time. Among them was Father Bressani, who was carried away captive by the Mohawks in 1644; but he says nothing in his Relation[1] about the lake.

The map published by the Jesuits in 1664, indeed, has a dotted trail from the south end of Lake St. Sacrament to the Mohawk villages; yet the absurd form given to the lake shows that whoever made the map had never sailed upon its waters. The trail laid down was probably the course pursued by the Indians. Father Poncet,[2] who was made a prisoner by the Iroquois in 1652, is silent respecting the lake. Father LeMoyne, who wrote four years later, maintains the same reticence.

January 30, 1666, the French operations became active, and Courcelles, Governor of Canada, left Fort St. Theresa to attack the Mohawks near the banks of the Hudson, but he returned February 12, without inflicting much injury upon the enemy. Later in the year, about the 1st of July, Sorel marched on the same errand, and while on his way met a deputation of Indians who were going to Montreal to effect a peace. Accordingly he returned, and on the 12th of the

(1) — Col. Doc., ix. 46. *Relations des Jesuites*, 1665, Vol. iii. p. 6.
(2) — ib., 1653, Vol. p. 11.

month a treaty was made with the Oneidas, it being agreed to "open a trade and commerce by the Lake du Saint Sacrement."[1]

September 14, Tracy, then Viceroy of Canada, finding the Mohawks extremely troublesome, sent the Governor, Courcelles, with a considerable force, to destroy their forts and villages. Tracy himself joined the expedition. Considerable success attended their efforts, though both the Viceroy and the Governor were disabled by hardship, and were carried back the most of the distance by their men, reaching Montreal in fifty-three days from the time they set out. The route taken by these expeditions is not noted with accuracy, yet it is highly probable that they passed over Lake St. Sacrament.

In 1668 Fathers Fremin, Pierron, and Bruyas went up Lake Champlain, and passed south from Ticonderoga by land. Near by the Indians showed them a place where some water-dwellers exchanged flints for tobacco. We give a translation of the account as narrated by the Fathers themselves. They say:

"We arrived at three-fourths of a league from the rapids, where Lake St. Sacrament empties. We halted at this place without knowing the reason, except that we saw our Indians pick up at the water's edge, gun-flints almost completely cut. We did not

(1) — Col. Doc.; Vol. ix. p. 46; iii. p. 123.

then give it any attention, but we subsequently learned the mystery, for our Iroquois told us that they never failed to halt at that place to pay homage to a nation of invisible men, who dwelt there at the bottom of the water, and were engaged in preparing gun-flints almost ready for use, for those who passed, provided they rendered them their obeisance by offering them some tobacco. If they gave much they gave the stones liberally. These water-men join canoes like the Iroquois; and when their great chief plunges into the water to enter his palace, he makes such a loud noise that it fills with terror the minds of all those who are not aware of his great genius."[1]

The Indians conversed on the subject very seriously; but the good Fathers explain that these stones, so useful in striking fire, were thrown up by the waves during the storms, and that the invisibles aforesaid have nothing to do with the matter.

The reverend Father says in the Relation, that while he stopped on an island on Lake Champlain, the rest went forward, the boatmen "landing at the end of the Lake du St. Sacrement, and preparing for the portage. Each one loads himself with baggage and canoes, in which, re-embarking, [in Lake St. Sacrament] at last, after some paddle-strokes, we left them, joyful to have reached the end of the lake, whence there remained thirty leagues to make by land."

(1) — *Relations des Jesuites*, 1368. Vol. iii. p. 5.

The language of the Relation is here a little obscure, but he probably means that only a part of the Indians re-embarked. We are, however, informed that the Iroquois kept a regular guard at this point. They remembered the expedition of Tracy two years before, and "all the country of the Iroquois was then in apprehension of a new army, so that fourteen men were continually on the watch at the end of the lake to discover the march of the army and give prompt news to all the nation, that they might set ambushes in the woods to attack and cut us in pieces. But instead of enemies," says the Father, "we were angels of peace; and they, instead of lions, were servants, and helped us to carry our packages. We marched in their company by small days' journeys."[1]

We find nothing further of interest, until Waite and Jennings crossed the lake on their way to Canada, to negotiate for the return of the English, who were taken prisoners by the French and Indians at Hatfield and Deerfield, Massachusetts, September 19, 1677. Under date of December 13, following, it is said: "Securing, with some difficulty, an Indian guide on whom they could rely, they proceeded to Lake George, where, finding a canoe, they crossed to the outlet of that lake in three days."[2] From thence they went on to St. John's, and at once found a part of the prisoners.

(1) — *Relations des Jesuites*, 1668. Vol. iii. p. 6.

(2) — Attack on Hatfield and Deerfield. Bradford Club, p. 32.

In 1690, hostilities being threatened between the French and English, the former at Montreal, Bancroft says, were frequently alarmed by reports that the Indians and colonists were building canoes and descending Lake St. Sacrament. But on June 21, of the next year, the English moved in earnest, and Major John Schuyler left Albany to attack Fort Lapraire. His force consisted of two hundred and sixty whites and friendly Indians, of which number no less than sixty-eight were killed and wounded before his return.

His expedition attracted much attention at the time, but resulted in little real good. During this expedition he sent scouting-parties out on Lake St. Sacrament, as it was then universally called, who ranged up and down its waters.[1] The expedition of Colonel Philip Schuyler to the same place, the following year, does not appear to have gone nearer the lake than Ticonderoga.

In 1692 Menteth, who commanded six hundred French, moved during the winter against the Mohawks living south of the Hudson, and defeated them with considerable loss. It is not so clear that he crossed the lake on his way south, yet he returned that way. The French report says, under date of March 2: "Came to sleep at Lake St. Sacrament; several of the Indians left us to hunt, and as they alone were

(1) — Col. Doc., Vol. iii. p. 800.

master of the prisoners, whom they did not guard very strictly, many of them escaped."

The next morning they moved on, and on the 4th they arrived at the place where they had previously deposited a quantity of provisions, which they found spoiled. This caused a "universal and most rigid fast." Some of the party boiled their moccasins with a few potatoes to satisfy their hunger. They reached Montreal on March 17.[1]

Queen Anne's war commenced in 1702, and continued until 1713. During this war the lake was used to some extent, and was, on the whole, the favorite route to Canada. It involved a portage at Ticonderoga, but it was considered by far the most healthy. The war, however, went on for about nine years before the quiet of the lake was seriously disturbed. At that time the colonists prepared to invade Canada, and on August 28 Colonel Nicholson marched with four thousand men, one half of whom were Germans and Indians. But he had scarcely reached the site of the present village of Caldwell, at the head of Lake St. Sacrament, when he heard of the failure of General Hill's expedition against Quebec, and received orders to return to Albany.

In 1745 hostilities again broke out with the French, who came down by the way of Lake Champlain and Fort Edward, in the course of the war destroying

(1)—ib., Vol. ix. p. 530.

Saratoga and capturing Fort Massachusetts, which was situated within the limits of Williamstown, Mass.

During this war the lake was visited by six hundred Dutch and friendly Indians. The former went on a scout down the lake in canoes, but did not meet with the enemy. Later, the French commander, Devillers, sent scouts to the lake, which he calls "Lake St. Laurent," who reported that they found camps and cabins sufficient to accommodate the above-mentioned number of men. The camps appeared as if they had not been left more than a month. Yet the war closed without any hostilities on the lake, which was next used to some extent by Indian smugglers. About this time a party of the Six Nations, who had deserted and established themselves near Montreal, seem to have monopolized the illicit trading between Albany and Montreal.[1] On one occasion they saved the life of a captive of another tribe, who had been taken to Crown Point, and carried him in their canoes across Lake St. Sacrament to his home.

The next year General Johnson, aftewards Sir William Johnson, visited the lake with several tribes of Indians. He tells us in his account of the Oneidas, that this tribe often used a tree as a symbol of stability, but that their true symbol is a stone, called *Onoga.* His visit to the lake was marked only by the setting up of the Indian signs. He writes: "I went on Lake

(1) — Colden's Five Nations, Vol. ii. p. 121.

St. Sacrament in 1746, when, to show the enemy the strength of our Indian alliance, I desired each nation to affix their symbol to a tree, to alarm the French. The Oneidas," he says, "put up a stone, which they painted red."[1]

In the year 1749 Kalm, the Swedish traveller, intended to pass down the lake, but was finally obliged to go by the way of Whitehall, though he testifies that the common route at that time lay over St. Sacrament, which indicates that the lake was well known.

We find no record of anything of much interest in connection with the lake from this time forward, until the year 1755, when, on the 28th of August, General Johnson built a military road, and, marching to the lake, encamped at its head with a small army, designed to operate against Crown Point, and repel the aggressions of the French, who were now preparing to assert their claims to a large part of the country. Immediately on his arrival he changed the name of the lake, and ordered that it should in the future be known as Lake George, "not only," as he said, "in honor of his Majesty, but to ascertain his undoubted dominion." This change was one that must ever be regretted, since no more beautiful or appropriate name could be suggested than that given by the devout Father Jogues, by which it was known for more than a century. "Lake Jogues," would be preferable to Lake George.

(1) — Doc. His., Vol. iv. p. 271.

When Johnson reached the lake he found the whole country covered with primeval woods, where, he says, though not with exact truth, "no house was ever before built, not a spot of land cleared." And while he was here engaged in making preparations to advance, the French general, Dieskau, made his appearance near the southern spur of French Mountain, with an army of two thousand men, a portion of whom were Indians.

A council of war was held on the morning of September 8, when it was resolved to send a force to meet the enemy. General Johnson at first proposed a somewhat small number of men for this service; but the old Mohawk sachem, "King Hendrick," a firm friend of the English, declared that the force was insufficient. "If they are to fight," said the chief, "they are too few; if to be killed, they are too many." Again, when Johnson proposed to divide the force into three parties, he took three sticks, and said: "Put these together and you cannot break them: take them one by one, and you can break them easily." Thus the question was settled, and Colonel Williams was placed in command of twelve hundred men, among whom was a body of Mohawk Indians under Hendrick.

Colonel Williams met the enemy at a brook four miles east of the lake, where the road to Glen's Falls now passes, and was unfortunately drawn into an ambush laid in the form of a half moon. The enemy at once opened a galling fire, under which the English force was mowed down like grass. The aged Hendrick, who rode horseback and directed the movements of his men, fell from his saddle, mortally wounded; and Colonel Williams was killed by a bullet, while standing on or near a rock, (which is still pointed out,) giving his orders. Colonel Whiting immediately succeeded to the command, and ordered the troops to fall back to the main body at the lake, from whence reinforcements had already been sent to their aid. This movement was accomplished with coolness, notwithstanding the previous blunder.

Dieskau rapidly followed, and at eleven o'clock reached the eminence where the slight earthwork called Fort Gage was afterwards built. Hoyt, who conversed with several soldiers engaged in the battle, gives an account of their impressions when they saw the disciplined Frenchmen appearing on the hill: "The regulars advanced in a column of platoons, then a novelty to provincial troops, and as the day was fine, their polished arms glittered through the tops of the intervening trees like masses of icicle, multiplying their number ten-fold."[1]

Johnson's camp was situated near the site of the ruins of Fort George, where he had formed a slight breastwork of logs, and was somewhat prepared to meet him. After a brief delay the enemy attacked

(1) — Antiquarian Researches, p. 276.

with much fury, and the battle raged for a period of five hours. Dieskau's Indians, however, feared the artillery of the English, and the French were unable, with all their exertions, to carry the position. Finally they gave up the attempt and retreated, the English jumping over the breastworks and pursuing for some distance. At sunset the remnant of the French army halted near the scene of the morning engagement, and while refreshing themselves there, were suddenly attacked by two hundred New-Hampshire men from Fort Edward, under Captain McGinnis. They were at once routed, and fled in dismay, leaving all their baggage, while the blood of the slaughtered men mingled with the water of a shallow pond, which has since been known as "Bloody Pond."

General Johnson was wounded early in the engagement at his camp, and retired to his tent, turning over the command to General Lyman, who stood in the most exposed positions, coolly giving his orders and cheering on the men, until the victory was secured. Still, Johnson did not have the magnanimity even to mention Lyman in his despatches, though in his tent he admitted the great value of his services. A conspiracy[1] was even formed among certain of the officers to accuse Lyman of *cowardice*. The conspiracy failed, but that brave man was kept from the enjoyment of his just reward. On the other hand General Johnson

(1)—Review of Mil. Operations in N. A., 1755-6. Series B, p. 64.

obtained great credit, and, in addition to the grant of a large sum of money by Parliament, was created a baronet.

In this engagement the intrepid Dieskau was wounded[1] and taken prisoner. His motto — *Valor wins* — signally failed in this instance. His whole army might have been either destroyed or captured, if the advantage gained had been followed up. Lyman strenuously advocated this policy, but Johnson thought it unsafe.

The troops engaged were chiefly from New England, New York furnishing only eight hundred. The loss was estimated at about three hundred in killed and wounded. The French lost from four to six hundred. They retreated to Crown Point and abandoned the campaign.

This was the first battle fought at Lake George. It was of great importance, both inasmuch as it rebuked the arrogant assumptions of the French, and taught them the hopelessness of seeking to divide the common interests. The result filled the whole country with the wildest joy, and the people everywhere began to take heart.

(1) — He was wounded twice. Some authorities say that the second shot — a severe one in his hips — was given by a renegade Frenchman; while others affirm that it was fired by one of the English, who, on approaching the wounded general to make him a prisoner, saw him put his hand in his breast as if to draw a pistol, whereas he was simply feeling for his watch. Dieskau died in Surenne, France, from the effect of his wounds, September 8, 1767.

Before leaving this subject, however, it may be proper to notice the spirit displayed by New York, then distracted by internal dissensions, and under the influence of the wrong leaders. The struggle going on was upon New-York ground, and was more especially designed for the protection of her people. The French power was in the ascendant, and an easy route by water was open between Montreal and the city of New York. The French fully announced their ambitious designs by the estabishment of a fort and colony at Crown Point twenty-five years before; and yet the people of New York, who at this time numbered not less than 55,000, seemed, on the whole, altogether too willing to yield their back to the smiter. "But," says Smith, in his history of New York, "a very different spirit prevailed in the eastern colonies; for, upon the southern defeat, Massachusetts added eight hundred, and Connecticut fifteen hundred, men to the forces already under General Johnson's command."[1] And when New York complained that the funds granted by Parliament to the Colonies were not justly divided, the agent said, among other things, in the way of reply, that the New-Englanders had "in a measure become the Swiss of the continent, in which quality they are not unacceptable."[2] In fact, this year Massachusetts had every fifth able-bodied man in the field.

(1) — Smith, Vol. ii. 261. (2) — ib.

It is true that the figures have been used to show that New York at this time contributed her full quota. Yet, in a crisis like that of 1755, there was no time to talk of *quotas*. The knife of the savage was at her throat, but there was no popular uprising; while Governor DeLancey, who affected considerable zeal, contented himself by sending the home government the preposterous story that New York had furnished three thousand men for Shirley's expedition to Niagara. It has been said that if the New-England men did the fighting they were *paid* for it. But if they were paid they were not paid by New York. It would be every way unjust to view the New-England troops as mercenaries. "Come," said Pomeroy, who represented the true spirit of New England, "come to the help of the Lord against the mighty; you that value your holy religion, and your liberties, will spare nothing, even to one half of your estate."

During the months of October and November, the troops were engaged in building a fort on the site now occupied by the Fort William Henry Hotel. It was named in honor of the Duke of Cumberland, brother of George III.

About this time a series of scouting expeditions was commenced. They were continued at intervals for two or three years. These expeditions were chiefly conducted by Rogers and his Rangers. He was often accompanied by Israel Putnam, who, in the Revolutionary army, ranked next to Washington.

October 14, Rogers, Putnam, and a soldier named Butterfield, embarked from Fort William Henry in a birch canoe for Crown Point, then in possession of the French. They landed nine miles from the outlet of the lake, and then travelled on foot to the vicinity of the fort where they lay in ambush. "At length," they say, "a frenchman Came out Towords us without his Gun and Came within fifteen Rods of Where we lay then I with another man Run up to him In order to Captivate him — But he Refused To Take Quorter so we Kill,d him and Took of his Scalp in plain sight of the fort then Run and in plain view about Twenty Rods and made our Escape."[1]

Such is the account signed by Rogers and Putnam; yet it is hard to believe that an unarmed man would refuse to take quarter, under the circumstances. We must rather put it down as one of those barbarous acts in which Rogers delighted.

One Captain Doolittle reports that he went on a scout to Ticonderoga, October 24, 1755, and that "after a tedias march over hills and holes we Indeavoured to Disscover ye french on this side ye Carrying Place but Could not hear of any of ye Choping or Shooting or Druming we went Down To the lake but Could not Disscover them." Crossing over to Ticonderoga he saw the French from a distance "light up ye fires and Beat ye Drums there appears to be about

(1) — Doc. Hist. N. Y., Vol. i. p. 175.

150 Tents [and] some small Boarden Housen." He afterwards attempted other observations, but a thick fog set in and "our Provision being spent Could tarrey no Longer God knows whether we Ever Get home if we Do I would Humbly Present these few Lines to Genl. Wm. Johnson."[1] This gives a fair idea of the literary character of these reports.

October 29, while the autumnal foliage of the lake was still in its glory, Robert Rogers and Israel Putnam went down the lake on a scout. On the 31st they "made a Discovry of a nomber of fires By night Scit-

FORT WILLIAM HENRY IN 1755.*

uated on a Point of Land on ye West Side of ye Lake," upon which they landed half a mile distant on the same side. The next morning they sent spies, who found four tents and some fires, whereupon Rogers sent back to Fort William Henry for reinforcements. He then took a boat and went down to within twenty-five rods of their fires, and discovered "a Small Fort with Several Small Log Camps within ye Fort which,"

(1)—Doc. Hist. N. York, Vol. iv. p. 175.

*The above view was cut by a soldier with a knife on a powder-horn, now in possession of the Maine Historical Society. It is a rude sketch, but doubtless correct. The island is Tea Island.

he says, "I Judged to Contain about 1-4 of an acre. Said Fort being open towards ye Water The rest Picketted." The next morning, Putnam, who had also gone over to reconnoitre, returned and reported that the enemy's sentry was posted twenty rods from their fires. Putnam went forward until he came "so nigh that he was fired upon by one of ye Centeries within a Rod of him, But unfortunately upon Preparing to Fire upon him fell into a Clay Pit and wett his Gun made ye Best retreat he was able, hearing ye Enemy Close to their Heels."[1] Afterwards the French rallied and endeavored to bring the English between a cross fire on the lake, but the latter detected the ruse, launched their batteaux, and opened a fire with the swivels or "wall peices," which were mounted on board. This had the desired effect, and "divers" of the French were killed. Putnam, who at this juncture was on the shore, was in great danger again, but, hurriedly launching his batteau, he joined the rest of the party, though not before the enemy, who made him a special mark, had "Shot thro' his Blanket in Divers Places." Finally, the English "put ym to ye Bush." When they "Got fairly into ye Lake," says the report, we "Lay upon Our Oars and Inquired after the Circomstances of ye Party. Found none Killed, but one Wounded which Gave Joy to all of us after so Long an Engagement which I Judge was near 2

(1) — N. York Doc. Hist., Vol. iv. p. 176.

Hours."[1] Putnam was now in training for the great work that he was afterwards to do in the War of the Revolution.

The report of James Connor of Colonel Cockcroft's regiment, who went on a scout November 5, shows the location of the stockaded fort which was the scene of Putnam's adventure. It appears that the French had now posted their advance guard on the east side of the Narrows. Connor found their fires on the night of November 5, when he fell back four miles and passed the next night in the mouth of a "little creek" on the east side — probably Shelving Fall Creek. The next day he went with two men over the hills on the east side of the lake, until he came opposite the fort on the west side, where the lake was about three hundred yards wide. Here they saw the French come down to the water and carry up timber on hand-spikes to the encampment, where they heard "workmen chopping and hammering," and saw "a breastwork round their encampment with pickets."[2]

This was probably what is called Friend's Point, near Anthony's Nose, at least if their estimate of distances is correct. Connor says that he built a fire on an island twenty miles from Fort William Henry, though, according to his own statement, this island must have been *south* of the Narrows, which are only

(1) — N. York Doc. Hist., Vol. iv. p. 176.
(2) — N. York Doc. Hist., Vol. iv. p. 178.

fourteen miles from the head of the lake. But his account is not perfectly clear, and possibly the location of the fort in question was at the more advantageous position afforded by Sabbath Day Point.

The scouting was carried on by the use of boats until the lake was frozen over, when it was continued by parties going over the ice with snow-shoes and sleds.

In 1756 the Earl of Loudon assumed the command of the English forces in North America. His plan contemplated a general attack upon the Canadas. One portion of his army was designed to move against Niagara; another was to attack Fort du Quesne; a third was to cross the country from Cambridge and operate on the river *Chaudiere*, while the fourth was to attack Crown Point. In accordance with this plan, six thousand men were assembled near the head of Lake George to attack the latter position. The colonial authorities gave the command of this force to General Winslow, before Loudon reached New York; but when this came to his knowledge, he wished to supersede Winslow by Abercrombie, who was one of the regular officers. Before this and similar disputes could be settled, the season passed away, and the troops were sent back to Albany and New York.

It is universally conceded that Loudon was a weak and inefficient commander, and totally disqualified for the position in which favoritism placed him. If remarkable for anything, it was for his insolence and tyranny, of the which the citizens of New York had no small experience. Franklin, in his Autobiography,[1] gives us a view of his character. It appears that Franklin had occasion to visit Lord Loudon's office in New York, where he met a Mr. Innis, who brought the despatches of Governor Denny from Philadelphia, the answer to which he expected the next day. Meeting him a fortnight afterwards, Dr. Franklin expressed his surprise because he had not returned. Mr. Innis explained that he had called every day, but the despatches were not ready. "Is it possible," said Franklin, "when he is so great a writer? I see him constantly at his escritoire." "Yes," said Innis, "but he is like St. George on the signs; always on horseback, but never rides forward."

At one time Loudon had no less than fifty thousand troops under his command, of which large number fifteen thousand were from the Old Bay State, then not at all in danger. With this force, an able commander might have crushed out the entire population of Canada; and yet nothing was done for the country. This season, however, there was, as usual, more or less scouting, with frequent attacks by the French and Indians upon the English teamsters.

July 7, Rogers, being down the lake with his Rangers, took several French prisoners. This hard-hearted wretch coolly says in his official report, that

(1) — Sparks' Life, p. 219.

"one of the wounded could not march; therefore put put an end to him to prevent discovery."[1] The circumstances of the case fully prove that this barbarous act admitted no justification.

July 18, Rogers went into the camp, near Saratoga, "with eight captives and *four scalps*."[2]

But though Loudon did nothing during the summer, the cold season was not allowed to pass in quiet. March 18, 1757, a force of French and Indians under Rigaud, attempted to surprise Fort William Henry. After a careful examination of the position, Rigaud found that, owing to the vigilance of the garrison, it would be impossible to storm the fort. Accordingly, he turned his attention to the destruction of the batteaux and other vessels, in which attempt he was, at first, not very successful. The next day he invested the fort on all sides, and called upon the commander to surrender, which he refused to do, saying that he should defend himself as long as possible. On the next night the French again resorted to the use of fire, and as the English opposed them with only a few shot and shells, they succeeded in burning more than three hundred batteaux, besides three sloops that were caught in the ice, and a storehouse filled with provisions and munitions of war. The absence of wind on that night saved the fort itself from destruction. The

(1) — Doc. Hist., Vol. iv. p. 185.
(2) — From the unpublished MS. Journal of the Rev. John Graham, Chaplain to the Connecticut troops.

next two nights the snow prevented all operations. On the 22d a final attempt was made upon a new sloop on the stocks, and whose bowsprit touched the bastion of the fort. In this they were successful. They also burned two other storehouses full of provisions, the hospital, a saw-mill, and more than twenty buildings.[1] On the 23d they decamped with a large amount of plunder.

Stark was in the fort at the time, and doubtless rendered good service; but the dramatic story of his saving the garrison from surprise, which is told in his Life, has no foundation in fact. The French did not attempt any assault, nor did they cut holes in the ice to dispose of the bodies of their slain, as that narrative claims.[2]

Emboldened by Rigaud's success, and influenced by the withdrawal of a large portion of the troops from the vicinity of the lake, who had been ordered away to Louisburg to share in the miserable failure of Lord Loudon, the commander-in-chief, Montcalm, determined to make one more attempt against Fort William Henry. Accordingly, on the 12th of July following, an army of nine thousand French and Indians, under Montcalm, left Montreal, fully equipped and with a formidable train of artillery.

The best account of the expedition is given by an eye-witness, Father Roubaud, who attended the Abe-

(1) — Col. Doc., Vol. x. p. 571.
(2) — Stark's Memoir of John Stark, p. 20.

nakis Indians as their priest and adviser. He says in his journal :[1] "We traversed the length of Lake Champlain, where the dexterity of the Indian furnished us with an amusing spectacle. Standing up in the bow of his canoe, with spear in hand, he darted it with wonderful address, and struck the large sturgeons, without their little skiffs, which the least irregular motion would have overturned, appearing to lean in the slightest degree to the right hand or the left. . . . The fisherman alone laid aside his paddle, but in return he was charged to provide for all the others, an office in whose duties he fully succeeded."

At the end of six days they came in sight of the fortifications at Ticonderoga, which place had been appointed as a general rendezvous for the forces. As the Indians approached the shore, they arranged themselves in the order of battle, each tribe under its own ensign. "Two hundred canoes thus formed in beautiful order," he says, "furnished a spectacle that caused even the French officers to hasten to the banks."

While the army lay at Ticonderoga, several preliminary engagements occurred on Lake George.

July 21, M. de St. Ours,[2] who was scouting at *Isle a la Barque*, with ten men, was attacked by five English barges, each carrying sixteen men. There were also one hundred English on the shore. Yet St. Ours made so good a defence that he was able to

(1) — Kip's Early Jesuit Missions, p. 144.
(2) — Col. Doc., Vol. x. p. 594.

escape with the loss of four — three slightly, and one mortally, wounded. The English loss, though exaggerated by the French, was probably considerable. This took place at Harbor Island, a little south of Sabbath Day Point.

July 23, M. Marin, who had been sent toward Fort Edward with one hundred and fifty men, mostly Indians, attacked the English outposts, and inflicted considerable loss, returning to Ticonderoga in safety, with no less than thirty-two scalps.[1]

July 26, Colonel John Parker, of the New Jersey regiment, was sent down the lake to reconnoitre, with a large party of men in boats. He was severely defeated, his force being completely cut in pieces. The French report says that about four hundred Indians, under M. de Carbiere, lay in ambush among the islands above Sabbath Day Point, and that when Colonel Parker's party had advanced too far to reteat, they attacked and defeated them with great slaughter. Only two barges escaped, and one hundred and eighty of the English were taken prisoners. This was acknowledged to be a severe disaster.[2] No less than a hundred and thirty-one were killed outright by the savages, who pursued them by land and water, mercilessly cutting them down. Only twelve were so fortunate as to escape both captivity and death. The prisoners were treated by the Indians with the most

(1) — Col. Doc., Vol. x. p. 591.
(2) — ib., 594. Penn's Archives, iii. 472. Kip's Early Jesuits, p. 152.

horrible barbarity. Father Roubaud, who gives an account of their atrocities, hardly dared to raise his head, expecting to see the English murdered before his eyes. Eventually his fears proved too true, and he was obliged to witness a spectacle more horrible than anything he had yet seen. He writes: "My tent had been placed in the middle of the camp of the Outaouacs. The first object which presented itself to my eyes on arriving there, was a large fire, while the wooden spits fixed upon the earth gave signs of a feast. There was indeed one taking place. But, O heavens! what a feast! The remains of the body of an Englishman was there, the skin stripped off, and more than one half the flesh gone. A moment after, I perceived these inhuman beings eat with famishing avidity of this human flesh; I saw them take up this detestable broth in large spoons, and apparently without being able to satisfy themselves with it. They informed me that they had prepared themselves for this feast by drinking from skulls filled with human blood, while their smeared faces and stained lips gave evidence of the truth of the story. What rendered it more sad was, that they had placed very near them some ten Englishmen to be spectators of their infamous repast."

The good man was powerless in the midst of these barbarities, and his appeals in behalf of the prisoners

(1) — Kip's Early Jesuits, p. 155.

were met by threats or gibes, the savages in one instance replying by offering him a piece of broiled human flesh. The prisoners were finally taken out of their hands by Montcalm, and sent under guard to Montreal.

On the first of August the main body of the army finally embarked on Lake George, the Chevalier Levi having marched, three days previous, down the west side of the lake, with a force of three thousand men, to protect those who were to follow on the water. The barges moved at two o'clock, P. M., and continued on until they left "Bald Mountain," (Rogers Slide) "to the north." Afterwards they "doubled a cape," (Anthony's Nose) and remained there during a severe storm which lasted six hours. They also "tarried a short time opposite to the Sugar Loaf." Father Roubaud says that they had not gone more than four or five leagues before they saw the proofs of their victory of the 24th. He writes: "There were the abandoned English boats, . . . but the most striking spectacle was the great number of the dead bodies of the English." Some were lying on the banks, and others were floating in the water.

The next morning at daybreak, Father Roubaud reached "the Bay of Ganasouke," (Northwest Bay, near Bolton,) and landed near de Levi's camp. At 10 o'clock de Levi marched forward, and at noon Montcalm moved on in the boats, now with the artillery in the van. In the evening two boats came down the lake from Fort William Henry, while the fleet was quietly winding along the dusky shore of "Sandy Bay." The English, perceiving the boat which belonged to the priests, then covered by an awning, steered for it unsuspectingly, as if too see what it was. As they approached, a sheep in the boat happened to bleat, when they took the alarm and endeavored to escape. The silence with which these operations had been conducted now ended, and twelve hundred savages suddenly flew to the pursuit, uttering the most horrid cries. The English first gained the land, deserted their boats, and fled to the woods; but not until four of their number had been killed and two taken prisoners. Father Roubaud says that when the account of the affair came to Montcalm, he was "charmed with the detail," and retired to make his plans for the next day. During the night, however, the army continued to move on, and reached the bay on the west side of the lake, near Fort William Henry. The artillery did not arrive until daybreak. It consisted of thirty-two cannon and five mortars, placed on platforms and borne on boats. In passing around the point, now called Cramer's Point, the batteries came in full view of the English, who were saluted by a "general discharge," which at "this time was mere ceremony, but it announced more serious matters."

The lake now resounded on all hands with the sounds of war, and everything was in motion. Fort William Henry, which the French sometimes called

Fort George, is described by Father Roubaud as "a square, flanked by four bastions; the curtains were strengthened with stakes, the trenches were sunk to the depth of eighteen or twenty feet." The walls were built of pine trees covered with sand. It mounted nineteen cannon and four or five mortars, while the garrison consisted of five hundred men. Seventeen hundred men occupied a fortified camp on the site of the ruins of Fort George. Montcalm landed on the west side of the lake, a short distance from the Lake House, and planted his batteries about seven hundred yards from the fort. He afterwards marched his regular troops to a position south of the fort, sending LeCorne with seventeen hundred French and Indians a little further on, where they could hold the road leading to Fort Edward. He then called upon Colonel Munroe to surrender, which demand he positively declined, as he was expecting immediate reinforcements from General Webb.

The siege lasted six days, during which time the fort was defended with great vigor, though without much loss of life on either side. Aid was earnestly requested of General Webb, whose troops were anxious to march to the rescue; but that cowardly officer finally decided to do nothing, and advised Colonel Munroe to surrender, who, seeing the hopelessness of his situation, agreed to capitulate. On the morning of August 9, at seven o'clock, a white flag was hoisted on the fort, and the surrender was made on the conditions that the garrison and the troops of the intrenched camp should march out with the honors of war, carrying away arms and baggage, and take with them one cannon, out of respect for the gallant defence they had made, and be furnished with a sufficient escort to Fort Edward. The French accordingly took possession at noon.

MONTCALM'S INDIANS.

Father Roubaud says that the terms of capitulation were submitted to the Indian chiefs, and that the articles were "universally applauded." Yet the compact was soon violated in the most horrible manner. The Indians were thirsting for blood and plunder, and even while the military ceremony of taking possession was going on, they penetrated through the embrasures of the fort into the casemates where the sick remained who could not march out of the fort with their companions. Some of these were among the first victims of savage cruelty. Father Roubaud witnessed their atrocities. He writes: "I saw one of these barbarians come forth out of the casemates, which nothing but the most insatiate avidity for blood could induce him to enter, for the infected atmosphere which exhaled from it was insupportable. He carried in his hand a human head, from which streams of blood were flowing, and which he paraded as the most valuable prize he had been able to seize." "But," he continues, "this was only a slight prelude to the tragedy of the morrow. Early in the morning the Indians began to assemble about the intrenchments, demanding of the English everything valuable which their greedy eyes could perceive. . . Nor were these requirements rejected by the English. They undressed, they stripped themselves, to purchase their lives." In the meanwhile the troops detailed to attend them on the march to Fort Edward, arrived and hastily formed, and the English began to file out. Says Father Roubaud: "Woe to those who closed the march, or the stragglers whom illness or any other reason separated from the main body! They were as good as dead, and their lifeless bodies soon covered the ground. . . . This butchery, which was at first only the work of a few savages, became the signal which transformed them into so many ferocious beasts. They discharged right and left heavy blows with their hatchets on those who came within their reach."

The number that fell in massacre, which filled the public mind with horror, varies greatly. Father Rou-

FORT WILLIAM HENRY HOTEL, CALDWELL.

baud says the number killed did not exceed forty or fifty, and adds: "The patience of the English in thus being contented to bow their heads to the weapons of the executioner, had the effect of shortly stopping the slaughter; but," he adds, "this did not turn the savages either to reason or equity. With fearful cries they engaged themselves in making prisoners."

The most of the accounts of this affair are wild exaggerations, the loss by death and captivity being placed at from five hundred to fifteen hundred. The first victims were the negroes and friendly Indians.[1] Speaking of the conduct of the former during the siege, one of the gunners wrote that "Our blacks behaved better than the whites."[2]

It would be difficult to exonerate Montcalm from all blame. He might have anticipated the events that occurred, and provided a sufficient safeguard. Le Corne, indeed, promised much in the way of protection to the English, but did little; and Carver, in his journal, mentions one French soldier who repulsed the English with abusive language when they appealed for protection. Yet it would be unjust to ignore the conduct of many of the French officers and soldiers who hazarded their own lives to save those of the English. Father Roubaud, the good priest of the

(1) — Hoyt says that one friendly Indian was *burned*. Ant. Researches, p. 290.
(2) — Col. Doc., Vol. vi. p. 1005.

Abenakis, was every way true to his profession, and labored earnestly to rescue the victims of savage cruelty. Among others, an infant separated from its mother, and had fallen into the hands of a relentless chief, who threatened it with death, unless ransomed by a *scalp*. This child was saved by the priest, who obtained a scalp from the stock of one of his own Indians. Father Roubaud, after getting possession of the child, carried it in his arms until he secured an English woman to act as its nurse. This woman had possession of the child but a few hours before its mother appeared, and, frantic with joy, clasped it in her arms.

That class of writers who furnish what may be called the Apocrypha of history, have delighted in wild exaggerations of this event. Drawing their material from the crudest sensation accounts of the day, they have not hesitated to record as facts the most improbable fancies. It is to be regretted that these accounts have crept into so many of our popular school histories, in one of which, now extensively used, we are informed that when Montcalm went away, he left the dead bodies of one hundred women shockingly mangled and weltering in their blood. The account is based upon a supposed letter of Putnam's[1] that was never written, and is of the same authority as that favorite but now exploded story of the school-boy,

(1) — Lossing's Field Book, Vol. i. p. 111.

which relates Putnam's descent into the wolf's den. National enmity has had much to do with these misrepresentations of Montcalm, who was every way a noble and humane man, as well as the ablest general of his day in all North America. Yet Smollet, in his History of England, did not hesitate to lay upon him (in addition to the massacre of Fort William Henry) the charge of giving up twenty English soldiers at the capture of Oswego, the previous year, to be butchered by the Indians. The charge, however, was thoroughly refuted at the time by an official investigation. The real author of the calamity of Fort William Henry, was Lord Loudon, who left the country exposed to the enemy.

The French delayed at Fort William Henry until August 16. On the previous night the fort was completely destroyed by fire, and while the ruins were still wreathed in smoke, Montcalm embarked and sailed down the lake. We conclude the account of this sad event in the language of Bancroft, who says: "The Canadian peasants returned to gather their harvests, and the lake resumed its solitude. Nothing told that living men had reposed upon its margin, but charred rafters of ruins, and here and there, on the hill-side, a crucifix among the pines to mark a grave."[1]

(1) — Bancroft's U. S., Vol. iv. p. 266.

COLONIAL DAYS.

CHAPTER VII.

> Fathers that like so many Alexanders,
> Have, in these parts, from morn till even fought,
> And sheath'd their swords for lack of argument.

Abercrombie's Expedition — The Preparations — The Voyage—The Attack—Defeat — Retreat — Amherst's Campaign — Capture of Ticonderoga.

ON THE following year another large army assembled at the head of the lake for the purpose of reducing Ticonderoga, and atoning for the acts of the French in the previous year. It was commanded by General Abercrombie, who had succeeded Lord Loudon. The campaign was planned with great confidence, and was inaugurated by scouts and skirmishes. On the 23d of June three separate detachments of Rogers' Rangers were sent out on the lake to reconnoitre; and Wednesday morning, July 5, at eight o'clock, the well-appointed army, now sixteen thousand strong, embarked in more than one thousand boats and batteaux. The day was one of unusual beauty, and scarcely a cloud obscured the sky. The fleet was arranged in complete military order. The Regulars sailed in the centre, the Provincials on the left, and the Light Infantry on the right of the advanced guard. The army was composed of fine and varied material. There was the sturdy, brown-faced farmer from Massachusetts and Connecticut, the determined, phlegmatic Dutchman, the hardy Englishman, the dashing Green-Mountain Boy, and the intrepid Scot. Lord Howe's regiment was one of much note, while its young commander was the "Lycurgus" of the whole army, being evidently of much more importance than Abercrombie himself.

The troops moved in high spirits, confident of an easy victory. But few more splendid scenes have ever been witnessed. The lines of boats adorned with streamers and flags, the troops clad in bright national colors, the burnished arms, the insignia of rank, the placid water, the long banks of oars dipping to martial notes, and the bright summer sun shining down upon all — formed a display of rare beauty. Not the least conspicuous part of the pageant was the Highland Regiment, of which old Duncan Campbell, of Invershaw, was Major. They could not have appeared to finer advantage even on their own bright Loch Katrine. Moving out from under the shadow of the French Mountain, they sail on towards the verdant isles, as if performing some holiday parade, reminding us of Scott's picture in the Lady of the Lake:

> "Now you might see the tartans brave,
> And plaids and plumage dance and wave;
> Now see the bonnet sink and rise,
> As his tough oar the rower plies;
> See flashing at each sturdy stroke,
> The wave ascending into smoke;
> See the proud pipers on the bow,
> And mark the gaudy streamers flow
> From their loud chanters down, and sweep
> The furrowed bosom of the deep,
> As rushing through the lake amain,
> They plied the ancient Highland strain."

The fleet continued on its course all day until dusk, when they reached Sabbath Day Point. Here they remained until eleven o'clock, waiting for three brigades and the artillery; and when these came up all moved on. At nine o'clock the next morning, they arrived at the foot of the lake, disembarked, and marched towards the French outworks. The route lay through dense forests; and being led by unskilful guides, the troops fell into some disorder, though still able to move on. Lord Howe led the right centre column, and when near Trout Brook, encountered the party of De Trepazec, less than three hundred in number, returning from a scout at Rogers' Slide. The French opened fire, and at the first volley Lord Howe was killed by a musket-ball. This threw the English into still greater confusion, but they rallied and attacked the French with such impetuosity, that nearly the whole body was either killed, wounded, or made prisoners. De Trepazec himself was mortally wounded. By this engagement the English gained nothing, except the forest, in which the principal portion of the troops passed the night. An officer who wrote a letter to a New-York paper, speaks of the action as highly discreditable to the English, who behaved badly, on the whole, and at one time came near being beaten by a mere handful of men.

The next morning, the 7th instant, Abercrombie withdrew the whole army to the landing-place. Colonel Bradstreet then went forward to rebuild the bridges. In the afternoon the main body of the army advanced to attack the French works. The assault was made with much spirit. Three times the English were repulsed, and as often returned to the charge; but "at the end of four hours, after a series of efforts that would have done honor to the soldiers of Cæsar, and an exhibition of valor that would have rivalled the most romantic days of chivalry," the army, about seven o'clock, was ordered to retire, though not before the English had fired by mistake upon one of their own corps. The night was spent at the landing, and Saturday morning the army embarked and rowed sadly up the lake, arriving at Fort George on Sunday evening, the 9th. No corps suffered more than the Highlanders, who, until now, with one exception,— the Battle of Fontenoy, in 1745,—had always been completely successful. Three times they mounted the French works, but not being supported they were forced to retire. Gray-haired Duncan Campbell fell at the head of his regiment, with John Campbell the commander, who was succeeded by Colonel Gordon Graham. During the battle, Abercrombie remained at a safe distance, and not a single piece of artillery was used by the English, who, under a general of respectable spirit and capacity, would have easily captured Ticonderoga. During the day Abercrombie ordered a movement against the enemy's left wing; but, after several boats had been sunk by the artillery of the French, the attempt was given up. This was a point that the most careful writers have failed to notice.[1]

This inglorious campaign was not terminated, however, before Colonel Bradstreet marched from the lake with twenty-seven hundred men and destroyed the French forts at Frontenac. When this had been accomplished, Bradstreet returned to the lake, and the bulk of Abercrombie's army went into winter quarters at Albany, New York, and elsewhere.

The next year Abercrombie was removed, and Lord Amherst was appointed in his place. This able general accomplished the reduction of Ticonderoga with but little loss of life. Before the campaign opened, Rogers was active on the lake with his Rangers. March 3, he left the head of the lake with three hundred and fifty-eight men, and proceeded on the ice to the Narrows, and afterwards went on to Ticonderoga. There he suffered a severe defeat from the French

(1)—N. Y. Col. Doc., Vol. x. p. 846.

and Indians, and returned by the way of Sabbath Day Point to Long Island, about five miles from Fort William Henry. At this place he encamped on the night of the 8th. The next day he went to Fort Edward, carrying the wounded on sleds.

June 21, General Amherst, accompanied by General Gage, moved to Lake George with a portion of the forces, composed of the Royal Highlanders and Provincials, who at once busied themselves in strengthening the camp.

On the 27th, some officers who were fishing at Diamond Island were surprised by the French scouts and nearly captured. July 1, troops to the number of fifteen hundred, under Colonel Montressor, were busy building a stone fort,[1] afterwards called Fort George, having in the meantime erected a temporary stockade. July 2, the enemy was extremely bold, notwithstanding the preparations of Amherst. On that day sixteen of the Jersey Blues had gone out from the fort to get brushwood for the ovens, and were attacked by two hundred and forty French, who killed and scalped six, wounded two, took four prisoners, and only four escaped. The French raised a loud halloo, and displayed the scalps in plain sight of the fort, and then ran to their canoes, which were only two miles from the head of the lake.[2]

July 3, the most of the articles buried by Abercrombie, at the close of the previous season, still

(1) — Knox Jour., Vol. i. p. 378. (2) — N. Y. *Mercury*, July 9, 1759.

remained undiscovered, though the French had found and raised a battery of eight pieces sunk in the lake. July 5, the "Halifax Sloop,"[1] mounting fourteen guns, which had been sunk to prevent capture, was successfully raised. July 12, Major Campbell and four hundred men embarked in batteaux and "proceeded to the islands on the lake to drive the enemy from

OLD HUT—1758.

thence," taking a floating battery of one twelve-pound gun. The French were driven away, and their "works and huts" destroyed and burned. The name of the

(1)—"On the 11th. instant was launched here, in 13 Days from laying the Keel, the Sloop Earl of Halifax, 51 Feet Keel, about 100 Tons Burthen, built by the direction of Commodore Loring and Col. Bagley. Her rigging being fitted, expected she will sail on a cruise on the Lake, in a day or two." Letter from Lake George, Aug. 21, 1758.

islands in question is not given. The French lost one canoe and all the men in it.

The preparations for the expedition having been made with great care, the army, composed of more than eleven thousand men, embarked in whaleboats and batteaux, on the morning of the 21st of July, and moved down the lake in four columns, the sloop Halifax sailing in the rear. The soldiers rowed by turns. An incredible amount of labor was spent in embarking, and some of the boats proved useless. One with a hundred barrels of powder sunk before leaving the shore; likewise a raft with two ten-inch mortars.

At ten o'clock the army reached the Narrows, and after pausing a short time, moved on with a fresh breeze and a hazy sky. At night the expedition moored,[1] the weather being rough with "a disagreeable tumbling sea." The next day was Sunday, July 23, but at daylight the fleet proceeded, and in a few hours reached the foot of the lake. The army landed without delay, and marched for Fort Ticonderoga. They reached the enemy's intrenchments after some light skirmishing, and the troops lay upon their arms all night. In the morning, seeing General Amherst drawing up his artillery, and finding that he had also launched batteaux in the lake, the French abandoned their intrenchments, of which the English took pos-

(1)—Probably below Sabbath Day Point.

session, in the face of a brisk fire, and began preparations for a siege; but at ten o'clock on the night of the 26th, some deserters from the French came in, announcing that the enemy had evacuated the fort and were retreating. Very soon after the magazine blew up and set the wood-work on fire. The flames rapidly communicated with the loaded guns and shell, and for a time created a continuous fire. The next morning a sergeant went into the fort, at the risk of his life, and hauled down the French flag. Thus the fort was taken with a loss of only thirty or forty in killed and wounded, which might have been done the year before.

But Lord Amherst, though a brave and faithful officer, failed to take advantage of his success. Instead of moving at once against the French, and to the aid of Wolfe, he delayed to repair the works at Ticonderoga and Crown Point, and prepare batteaux, until more than two months had slipped away, when the season was too far advanced to begin operations. The French army was not more than one fourth as large as his own, and Montcalm never seriously intended to hold Ticonderoga, where it was impossible for him to receive reinforcements, and yet they were allowed to escape down Champlain. Nevertheless, his victory brought comparative peace to the shores of Lake George, and ultimately removed the contest towards the Canadas, so that on September 21, Lieutenant-Governor DeLancey issued a proclamation calling upon the settlers to return once more to their homes, where they lived in quiet until the war of the Revolution.

In the meanwhile, many of those who had served in the wars applied to the colony of New York for grants of land around the lake. Among them was Rogers the Ranger, who, with twenty-five others, applied for twenty-five thousand acres of land on the west side of Lake George, extending from Fort William Henry to Tongue Mountain. It may also be noted, that here, in 1776, Rogers, being then a Tory, renewed the application to the British authorities, coolly proposing "Rogers' Mount," as the name of the grant.

April 20, 1773, Mr. Samuel Deall, a merchant of New York, who was much interested in building mills and improving the lands around Ticonderoga, petitioned for the exclusive right to establish a ferry across Lake George, though the right was not granted. He was associated in the improvements here with one Lieutenant Stoughton, who was drowned on the lake near the close of the year 1767, when his boat went to the bottom with all its valuable freight.

About this time the settlers had become quite numerous. As early as 1768, Mr. Deall had a small vessel on the lake called the "Petty Anger,"[1] which

(1)—This is probably a mistake of the printer. It should read "Petti-auga,"—a small vessel or ship. The following extract from Dunlap's New York, (Vol. ii,, Appen., p. 177,) gives a correct idea

was designed to traverse the lake, "if any freight offers worth going over." It was in charge of one John Jones, who lived at Fort William Henry.

The Indians came here in the summer season in considerable numbers, feeling that they had a tolerable right to the soil. They were not always peaceably tolerated, as appears from the following account of Levi Beardsley, who says his grandfather, before the Revolution, made annual excursions to the great forests bordering on Lake George, the favorite hunting-ground of the Iroquois. He tells that on one occasion, "coming near a swampy piece of ground, his companion remarked that game was plenty in that neighborhood, and asked him to walk with him to the edge of the swamp, where some one had shot a large buck a few days before. They repaired to the spot, where his companion pulled away a few pieces of rotten wood, that had been thrown on a large Indian, who lay there partly stamped in the mud. I have no suspicion," he says, "that my grandfather ever shot, or encouraged the shooting of Indians, but it is very certain, that he occasionally associated with those who indulged in this interesting business. Those times were perilous," he continues, "and conflicts frequent between the white and red man. . . . They were inev-

of this class of vessels, in one of which Mr. Vanderbilt began his career as a Staten-Island ferryman: "A perri augur or petty auga, a boat without keel, with two masts and two large sails, the lack of keel supplied by lee-boards — all these managed by one man, who was likewise helmsman, and very frequently drunk."

itable, and of no uncommon occurrence; for it was a question whether the red man alone should enjoy the game of the country."[1]

The handful of military stationed at Ticonderoga, were now chiefly useful in preserving the peace among the lawless inhabitants of the New-Hampshire Grants, which extended as far south as the head of the lake. Prominent among the New-Hampshire men, who, at times, invaded the territory of New York, was Colonel Ethan Allen, who often played the part of a swaggering brigand. The fortifications were now, also, in a bad condition. In 1768, Fort George was practically abandoned. In April, 1773, the fort at Crown Point caught fire, and the magazine, containing one hundred barrels of powder, blew up, completely destroying the works. The minutes of the Council at the close of the following September, say that Ticonderoga was in so ruinous a condition, that there was no accommodation for more than about fifty men. In 1774, Governor Tryon reported that "only a few men were kept at the south end of Lake George to facilitate the transportation of supplies to Ticonderoga and Crown Point;" from which it appears that the British authorities were but poorly prepared for the events about to take place.

(1) — Beardsley's Reminiscences, p. 16.
(2) — Doc. Hist., N. Y., i. p. 518.

REVOLUTIONARY SCENES.

CHAPTER VIII.

FORT GEORGE — NORDBERG — SCHUYLER — SICKNESS — BURGOYNE — INVASION OF NORTHERN NEW YORK — PEACE.

> Wake, soldier, wake! — thy war-horse waits
> To bear thee to the battle back.

PASSING on to the year 1775, we find the country in the excitement of a revolution, which was inaugurated at Lake George by an earthquake, which did no harm. But the lake at once became the theatre of exciting events, as it still formed a part of the central route between Albany and Montreal. The English felt the importance of keeping possession of this route, and one of their journals of that date says, that, in event of its being held by the Americans, the British troops would be brought around to New York by water, as another campaign could not be thrown away in "frog-battles" on the lakes. Yet Burgoyne ultimately thought differently.

The Americans, however, were on the alert, and the New-Englanders resolved on the seizure of Ticonderoga, which was the key of the whole position. This was accomplished by Benedict Arnold and Ethan Allen, on the morning of May 10, without the loss of a man. And serious efforts were recently made to show that a similar exploit was performed at Fort George, two days afterward. One account, which not long since appeared, stated that on the reception of the news of the Battle of Lexington, one Daniel Parks, of Queensbury, raised a band of volunteers, and afterwards marched to Fort George, which, together with "Fort Gage," was garrisoned by two companies of artillery. On his arrival at the fort his demonstrations were so impressive as to cause the garrison to flee down the lake to Diamond Island, where they intrenched. The commander, it appears, was left behind, and, on surrendering his sword, is represented as telling Parks that his neck would "stretch" for "this thing." According to the representations given, this alleged action of Daniel Parks was quite as meritorious as the capture of Ticonderoga. But though it may seem a pity to spoil a story, we, nevertheless, have abundant means for proving the account a fabrication.

It has already been shown that the fort was abandoned eight years before this time, while Governor Tryon reported that the year previous only a few men lived there to forward supplies; while "Fort Gage," the little earthwork on a neighboring eminence, which was probably erected in 1759 by General Amherst, never possessed a garrison or a gun. The position at the head of the lake had at this period lost its former importance, and therefore it is not *reasonable* to suppose, that while no effort was made to strengthen more commanding posts, Fort George had been reinforced by two companies of artillery. Indeed, this was a force superior to all the other garrisons combined. Besides, the intercepted despatches of General Carlton to General Gage, show that the total number of British troops in Canada at this time numbered only seven hundred and twenty-five, including the garrisons at Ticonderoga, Skenesborough, and Crown Point. The condition of affairs at the lake, prior to 1775, would constitute a sufficient denial of the story of Parks.

And the documentary evidence of the year 1775, goes to show that everything remained unchanged, except that fewer persons lived near the fort. May 12, there were only two persons at the fort, who were engaged in the express business. The fort had no commander, but the lake had a nominal "Governor"; and the apprehension and dismissal of this person has furnished the only ground for the romance of Daniel Parks. The person thus treated was Mr. John Nordberg,[1] formerly an officer in the English army. In

(1) — Mr. Nordberg was a native of Sweden, where he was born in 1710. Favoring the French faction there, he was persecuted, and left

1774, as a reward for his military services, he was appointed "Governor" of Lake George, an office without duties. The terms of his appointment left him at liberty to reside *anywhere* in America. At the period referred to, he was living, not in Fort George, but in a cottage near by, where, being an old man, and an invalid, he passed his time after the manner of a hermit, gladly escaping from the political discussions of the day. And the records show that Mr. Nordberg was actually visited by a party who went through the form of an arrest, but afterwards gave him a passport to New Lebanon. The person who took this responsibility was Captain Bernard Romans, a

Sweden. He entered the British service in January, 1758, as one of the foreign officers of the Royal Americans. He served in the French war, receiving two wounds. He afterwards went with his battalion to the West Indies. In 1773 he went to England, being invalidated, but returned to America the next year as Governor of Lake George. May the 12th, (*not* April, as Governor Tryon says, in Col. Doc., Vol. viii. p. 597,) he was apprehended at his cottage and sent away. December 15, the Provincial Congress gave him liberty to remove to England; but it appears that he remained in New York, where he died October 9, 1782. See Jour. Prov. Congress of N. Y., Vol. i. p. 220. We also find the following in Henry's travels at Lake Superior, 1771, p. 231: "Mr. Norburg, a Russian gentleman, acquainted with metals, and holding a commission in the sixtieth regiment, and then in garrison at Michilimackinac, accompanied us on this latter expedition. As we rambled, examining the *thods*, or loose stones, in search of minerals, Mr. Norburg chanced to meet with one, of eight pounds weight, of a blue color, and semi-transparent. This he carried to England, where it produced in the proportion of sixty pounds of silver to a hundred weight of ore. It was reposited in the British Museum. The same Mr. Norburg was shortly afterward appointed to the government of Lake George."

member of the Connecticut Committee appointed to take possession of "Ticonderoga and its dependencies."[1]

Several writers, in giving an account of the action of the Connecticut Committee, state that Romans left his associates at Bennington, and did not appear until he came to Ticonderoga, May 14. Mott says in his journal: "Mr. Romans left us and joined us no more; we were all glad, as he had been a trouble to us, all the time he was with us."[2]

It appears that Romans, finding it impossible to manage the other members of the Committee, with reference to the surprise of Ticonderoga, decided to seize Fort George on his own account. This was certainly included in the instructions of the Committee, and it was the only thing left him to do, as the surprise of Skenesborough was already provided for. Therefore, without consulting any one, he went to the head of the lake, took possession of what time and the weather had left of Fort George, and sent away Mr. Nordberg to New Lebanon.

Romans felt that the capture of an abandoned fort was not a thing to boast of, and therefore gave no publicity to his action. It has never even been mentioned in connection with the capture of Ticonderoga.

Daniel Parks *may* have followed in the train of Captain Romans, and may also have been a member of the garrison, when it was soon after found necessary

(1) — See Appendix. I. (2) — Conn. Hist. Col., Vol. i. p. 169.

to maintain a small force at this point; but that he raised troops for the capture of what he knew to be a ruinous and deserted work, is not to be supposed for a moment. Mott says in his Journal, that they sent men "to waylay the roads" leading to "Fort Edward and Lake George,"[1] for the express purpose of *preventing* alarm in what was, on the whole, a Tory neighborhood. Indeed, it has not been proved that Parks was on the ground at the time in *any* capacity. Still, there is a monument in the burying-ground at Sandy Hill which states that he was the man to whom the British officer surrendered Fort George. But, as shown from the above account, the fort had neither garrison nor commander. The story is a myth.

From a document[2] never before published, we learn the outside cost of the work of Captain Romans, which probably was less than thirty shillings. The document is also of value, in showing what disposition was made of the British prisoners taken at Ticonderoga.

Soon after Mr. Nordberg's dismissal, the colonial authorities found it necessary to establish a small garrison at Lake George, chiefly for the purpose of forwarding supplies to the troops operating on Lake Champlain.

May 25, it was voted by the Continental Congress to leave the authorities of New York to decide what troops should be stationed at Lake George. May 30, New York not having raised any troops, Governor

(1) — Conn. Hist. Coll., Vol. i. p. 169. (2) — See Appendix. II.

Trumbull, of Connecticut, ordered one thousand men, under Colonel Hinman, to Ticonderoga, where four hundred of them arrived about the middle of June. July 1, there were upwards of one hundred men stationed at each end of the lake.

Major General Philip Schuyler, of New York, having been appointed to the command of the Northern department, went down Lake George, July 17, arriving at Ticonderoga the next morning, when he formally superseded Colonel Hinman, who had previously displaced Benedict Arnold from the command. We may judge of the degree of discipline which was maintained at this time by the following extract from his letter to Washington. He writes:

"About ten, last night, I arrived at the landing-place, at the north end of Lake George, a post occupied by a captain and one hundred men. A sentinel on being informed I was in the boat, quitted his post to go and awaken the guard, consisting of three men, in which he had no success. I walked up and came to another, a sergeant's guard. Here the sentinel challenged, but suffered me to come up to him, the whole guard, like the first, in the soundest sleep."[1]

July 24, there were two hundred and thirty-three men of Colonel Goose Van Schaick's regiment, at or near Fort George. About this time the soldiers at Fort George were in a mutinous condition, and suffered greatly for the want of blankets, so that

(1)—Letters to Washington, Vol. i. p. 6.

several of their officers, when visiting at Albany, professed that they did not dare to return without them.

The operations of the Americans this year were conducted by Schuyler and Montgomery. The army was supplied with food and war material by the transports on Lake George. Early in the campaign Schuyler was forced by sickness to leave the field, and Montgomery captured Fort St. John and Montreal. In the attack upon Quebec he failed, after a siege of three weeks, which ended in an assault that cost his own life, and the surrender of a portion of the troops who penetrated into the lower town. The remaining portion of the invading army wintered at Sillery. On the first of April, 1776, Wooster, who had succeeded to the command, made another attempt upon Quebec, but failed. Soon after the English received reinforcements, and the Americans were obliged to retire.

A more efficient commander being needed in Canada, General Thomas was appointed, and his army was made independent of the department under Schuyler. He at once moved toward the scene of action, hoping to stay the tide of defeat. April 17, he passed down the lake, and the next day forty batteaux started, carrying five hundred troops. On the 19th, a person at the lake, writing, says: "The whole of the troops that are now on the lake and here, will amount to upwards of fifteen hundred men; so that I think we shall make a very respectable figure before Quebec when we all arrive." They never arrived; and General Thomas died of the small-pox.

At this time Benjamin Franklin, Samuel Chase, and Charles Carroll reached the lake. They had been appointed by Congress, as Commissioners, to proceed to Canada and negotiate with the authorities there. They were accompanied in this mission by the Rev. John Carroll, afterwards the Roman Catholic Bishop of Baltimore. The account of this trip across Lake George is given by Charles Carroll in his journal.[1] Portions of the journal are of sufficient interest to be reproduced here:

"April 19, 1776. We embarked about one o'clock, in company with General Schuyler, and landed in Montcalm's Bay, about four miles from Lake George. After drinking tea we again embarked, and went about three or four miles further; then landed (the sun being set) and kindled fires. The longest of the boats, made for transportation of troops over Lakes George and Champlain, are thirty-six feet in length and eight feet wide; they draw about a foot of water when loaded, and carry between thirty and forty men, and are rowed by the soldiers. They have a mast fixed in them, to which a square sail or blanket is fastened, but these sails are of no use, unless with the wind abaft, or nearly so. After we left Montcalm's Bay, we were delayed considerably in getting through

(1) — Baltimore, 1860. Published by the Maryland Hist. Society.

the ice; but, with the help of tent-poles, we opened ourselves a passage through it into free water. The boats fitted up to carry us across, had awnings over them, under which we made up our beds, and my fellow-travellers slept very comfortably. We left the place, where we passed the night, very early on the 20th.

"20th. We had gone some miles before I arose; soon after I got out of bed, we found ourselves entangled in the ice. We attempted, but in vain, to break through it in one place, but were obliged to desist and force our passage through another, which we effected with much difficulty. At eight o'clock we landed to breakfast. After breakfast, the general looked to his small boat; being desirous to reach the landing at the north end of Lake George, we set off together; but the general's boat, and the other boat with part of the luggage, soon got before us a considerable way. After separating, we fell luckily in with the boat bringing the Montreal and Canada mail. Dr. Franklin found in the mail a letter for General Schuyler. When we had weathered Sabaty point, we stood over for the western shore of the lake, and a mile or two below the point we were overtaken by the general, from whom we learned the cause of his delay. Mr. Chase and myself went on board the general's boat, and reached the landing-place at the south [north] end of Lake George, nearly two hours before the other boats. Lake George lies nearly north and south. . . . Its shores are remarkably steep, high, and rocky, (particularly the east shore), and are covered with pine and cedar, or what is here termed hemlock; the country is wild and appears utterly incapable of cultivation; it is a fine deer country, and likely to remain so, for I think it never will be inhabited. I speak of the shores, and am told that the country inland resembles these.

"The season was not sufficiently advanced to admit of catching fish, a circumstance that we had reason to regret, as they are so highly prized by connoisseurs in good eating, and as one of our company is so excellent a judge of this science."[1]

The Commissioners accomplished no good by their visit to Montreal, and the party returned by South Bay and Fort Edward.

May 31, General Schuyler was now at the lake, having his headquarters at Fort George. About this time he was visited by Mr. Graydon, who came to the lake to bring money for the troops. Speaking of the journey between Fort Edward and the lake, he says: "It was almost an entire wood, acquiring a deeper gloom, as well from the general prevalence of pines, as from its dark, extended covert, being pre-

(1) — Mr. Carroll writes under date of April 5, when the Commissioners were ascending the Hudson: "Just before we doubled Cape Anthony's Nose, Mr. Chase and I landed to examine a beautiful fall of water. Mr. Chase, apprehensive of the leg of mutton being boiled too much, was impatient to get on board."

sented to the imagination as an appropriate scene for the 'treasons, stratagems and spoils' of savage hostility."[1]

He was received at the lake by Schuyler with great cordiality and respect, and appears to have heartily approved his tactics in dealing with the New-England troops under his command. Graydon bears testimony to his irritability, but thinks that the New-England men deserved the contemptuous treatment which they received at his hands, a very striking instance of which is recorded. Eventually, however, his policy failed. As Greene observes: "New-England men could not persuade themselves that the man who, in his official intercourse with them, could not command his 'peevishness' was qualified to command them."[2] This remark is conceived in the spirit of that ancient declaration, which teaches that the ability to rule one's spirit is a truer mark of greatness than the capacity to take a city; yet, if mutual forbearance had been exercised, Schuyler might, perhaps, have continued in command of this department to the end, and finally achieved the victory that afterwards crowned the efforts of Gates.

A polished gentleman of the old school, General Philip Schuyler carried all his high-bred courtliness into the camp, where he found it difficult to recognize the worth of those New-England men, who, at times,

(1) — Memoirs, p. 142.
(2) — Life of General Greene, Vol. i. p. 483. Graydon, p. 143.

like many of their fellow patriots of New York, possessed noble and disinterested natures, veiled under a rude garb and ordinary mien. Hence, the mutual dislike and open hostility which afterwards had so much to do in removing this able soldier and wise statesman from the command of the Department of the North.

But let us not anticipate events. July 17, General Gates, who, a month previous, had succeeded Thomas in command of the army, which had now been driven far out of Canada, issued an order from his head-quarters at Ticonderoga, forbidding "the wanton waste of powder" at Fort George. Powder was at this time scarce, and a rebuke was perhaps needed, yet Gates, having entered the department of his superior, had no authority to administer it. Nine days before, the question of jurisdiction had come up in Congress, and the decision was against Gates, who was ordered to act in harmony with Schuyler, and restrict the use of his authority to his own immediate command.

October 1, Schuyler wrote to General Gates, saying that a blow at Fort George was probably meditated by the English, to destroy the communications of the American forces, and recommended a reinforcement. No harm came, however; yet in the following November the New-York Committee of Safety wrote that the Tories had a plan to seize and hold Fort George, in connection with the Indians and Canadians. This, likewise, was simply an ungrounded fear, as on the ninth of the same month General Gates writes somewhat tartly to Colonel Gansevort, because he kept the boats and provisions at Fort George, and sent forward no flour, telling him that "there is not an enemy within a hundred miles of the post."

Several writers have stated that about this time a severe battle was fought by a party of American militia of Saratoga county,[1] who met a band of Tories and Indians near Sabbath Day Point, when the former achieved a victory. Yet this story does not appear in print until a very recent date. The following paragraph from Mr. Neilson's little book on Burgoyne's campaign, contains the *only* authority found thus far. He says, speaking of events at this time, "My [step] grandfather, at the head of fifty men, had a desperate encounter with about eighty Indians and Tories at Sabbath Day Point, in which the enemy were defeated, with a loss of forty killed and wounded."[2]

Unfortunately, however, the chronicles of the day, which gave minute accounts of every skirmish, say nothing whatever either about such an engagement or victory. The only traces found by the author, of a conflict at this place appear in a fragment of a manuscript letter now in the State archives at Albany. It was written by "J. Deane, Indian Interpreter" to

(1) — Lossing's Field Book, Vol. i. p. 116.
(2) — Burgoyne's Campaign, p. 85.

General Schuyler, and bears date of June 25, 1777. In the course of his remarks he speaks of "the warriors of Aghmejasne, who took a party of our people at Sabbath Day Point."[1] In the absence of reliable testimony, we shall therefore feel obliged to receive with extreme caution Nelson's account of a victory at the above place. Lossing repeats Nelson's story, but gives no authority. So important an engagement would certainly have been mentioned in some document or newspaper of the day.[2]

It would be improper to pass over this year without speaking of the severe sickness which prevailed. When the army under Gates was obliged to retreat up Champlain to Ticonderoga, the sick were transported over Lake George to the hospitals established around the fort at its head. This site was selected on account of its genial atmosphere and general advantages. On the 14th of July there were no less than three thousand sick men lying at this place,[3] many of whom were suffering from small-pox and typhus fever. Between the 12th and 26th of July, fifty-one men were here consigned to the grave. What is now the village of Caldwell was one great charnel house. The circumstances were rendered worse by the fact, that the hospitals were extremely destitute of all those means and appliances which in our own day go so far

(1)—Miss. Papers, 1777, Vol. xxxviii. p. 20.

(2)—The author has not been able to learn even the *name* of the person who commanded in this alleged fight.

(3)—American Archives, Vol. i., Series v. pp. 232-237-651.

to alleviate human misery. The sufferings of the troops at Valley Forge could not be compared with the misery of our patriotic troops on the shore of this beautiful lake.

Among those prostrated by disease and borne to this place, was General James Wilkinson, afterwards the co-laborer of Aaron Burr, and Baron de Woedtke.[1] Wilkinson says: "There at Fort George, in spite of medical aid, I was reduced to the last extremity; every hope of my recovery had expired; I was consigned to the grave, and a coffin was prepared for my accommodation."[2] Yet he recovered from this sickness, and in course of time the diseases abated, and the hospitals were cleared, though too many of them had been rendered tenantless by Death.

Towards the close of the season, Trumbull passed up the lake from Ticonderoga, in a boat with General Gates, under whom he was serving as adjutant-general. He gives in his journal a beautiful picture of a mountain on fire, a scene well adapted to impress the mind of the embryo artist, who was about to lay aside the sword for the mahl stick. He writes: "My taste for the picturesque here received a splendid gratification. Some of the troops who had passed before us

(1)—Baron de Woedtke was many years an officer in the Prussian army. He came to America, and March 16, 1776, was appointed brigadier-general, and ordered to Canada. He died at Lake George, at about the close of July, and was buried with the honors due to his rank. Washington's Writings, Vol. iv. p. 6.

(2)—Memoirs, Vol. i. p. 86.

had landed on the west shore of the lake and lighted fires for cooking. The season was cold and dry — the leaves had fallen in masses — the fire had extended to them, and spread from ledge to ledge, from rock to rock to the very summit, where it was from seven hundred to a thousand feet high. In parts the fire crept along the crevices of the rock; at times an ancient pine tree rose up a majestic pyramid of flame; and all this was reflected in the pellucid surface of the lake, which lay like a beautiful mirror in the stillness of the dark night, unruffled by the oars of our solitary boat, and these were frequently suspended that we might enjoy the magnificent scene."[1]

Winter closed in gloomily upon the country, as well as upon the lake. About New-Year's day, the lake was frozen over, and navigation ceased. The cold season passed away without any event of importance occurring in the various garrisons. But when the of 1777 opened, the whole aspect of affairs underwent a change.

In order to render the operations of the army more effective, Congress, May 22, confirmed General Schuyler in his command, and added to his former jurisdiction, including Ticonderoga, Fort Stanwix, Albany, and their dependencies.[2] Thus Gates was put out of the field. General St. Clair was then placed in command at Ticonderoga. Eventually, that

(1) — Trumbull's Reminiscences, p. 37.
(2) — Journal Congress, Vol. iii. p. 183.

DEER BY THE BRINK OF STILL WATER.

officer, acting on his own responsibility, decided, in view of the impending peril, to evacuate the post. For this act Schuyler was severely blamed, yet he was in no wise responsible; while St. Clair himself was afterwards fully acquitted by a military court. The day after the evacuation of Ticonderoga, Schuyler, writing to Washington from Fort Edward, says, " I have not been able to learn what is become of General St. Clair and the army."[1]

St. Clair executed this movement on the night of July 6, sending one regiment and the sick to Whitehall, while the rest of the troops marched by the new road through the woods to Hubbardstown. The British, under General Frazer, took possession, and thus the evacuation of all points on Lake George became necessary. St. Clair's retreat having become known, preparations were made in season to leave Fort George; and when the Americans deserted that work they took all their baggage and stores, and set the fort on fire. The match was applied July 16, and Major Yates marched away to Fort Edward, with seven hundred men. Burgoyne, who was then moving victoriously southward, thus writes of the affair:

"The garrison of Fort George in manifest danger of being cut off by the direct movement from Skenesborough to Hudson's River, took the measure I expected of abandoning the Fort, and burning the vessels, thereby leaving the lake entirely free. A detachment

(1)—Washington's Writings, Vol. iv. p. 491.

of the King's Troops from Ticonderoga, which I had ordered to be ready for that event, with a great embarkation of provisions, passed the lake on the same day that I took possession of this communication by land." Schuyler, in his letter to Washington, before referred to, says that there were "no carriages to remove the stores from Fort George," which he expected would be immediately attacked. Yet it appears that Colonel Gates found means seven days after to bring away every thing in safety. Schuyler also justified the giving up of Fort George, on which point Washington suspended his opinion, merely remarking that others had informed him "that a spirited, brave, judicious officer, with two or three hundred good men, together with the armed vessels you have built, would retard Burgoyne's passage across the Lake for a considerable time, if not render it impracticable, and oblige him to take a more difficult and circuitous route." To this Schuyler replies: "The fort was part of an unfinished bastion of an intended fortification. The bastion was closed at the gorge. In it was a barrack capable of containing between thirty and fifty men; without ditch, without wall, without cistern; without any picket to prevent an enemy from running over the wall. So small, as not to contain above one hundred and fifty men, commanded by ground greatly overlooking it, and within point blank shot; and so situated that five hundred men may lie between the bastion and the Lake, without being seen from this *extremely* defensible fortress. Of vessels built there, one was afloat and tolerably fitted; the others still upon the stocks; but, if the two had been upon the water, they would have been of but little use, without rigging and guns."[1]

The same poor condition prevailed at Fort Edward, where Schuyler had only fifteen hundred men, with only two pieces of small iron cannon, all the artillery having been sent to the southern department by order of Washington. We may easily imagine what must have been the real state of affairs. An extract from a letter written by Governeur Morris to John Jay, when at Valley Forge, January, 1780, says: "Our troops, — *heu miserors.* The skeleton of an army presents itself to our eyes in a naked, starving condition, out of health, out of spirits. *But I have seen Fort George,*" he adds, "*in the summer of* 1777."[2]

Lake George being wholly given up by the Americans, it now became a part of the British line of communication with Canada. Colonel Anstruther was the commandant.

It is almost universally conceded, however, that he erred greatly in failing to bring his army by this route after the surrender of Ticonderoga. If he had done this, instead of moving by the way of South Bay, the result would doubtless have been far different. The general plan of the campaign was esteemed

(1) — Washington's Writings, Vol. iv. p. 494.
(2) — Life of Governeur Morris, Vol. i. p. 154.

judicious, and it gained the approval of King George himself. But that monarch saw the dangers of South Bay, and earnestly recommended the route by Lake George. In revising the plan he says: "If possible, possession must be taken of Lake George, and nothing but an *absolute impossibility* of succeeding in this, can be an excuse for proceeding by South Bay and Skenesborough."[1] Still, Burgoyne afterwards made as good a use of the lake as he was able to, and by this route he brought reinforcements and supplies. Depots were formed at both Fort George and Diamond Island, though eventually all of the stores were accumulated at the latter place.

But the British were not allowed to hold the lake unmolested. While Burgoyne was busy prosecuting his campaign in the direction of Saratoga, an expedition was sent by General Lincoln to his rear. This expedition was placed under the command of the ever-active Colonel John Brown, who surprised the outworks of Ticonderoga, and met with considerable success.[2] He then embarked with his forces in some captured vessels, and sailed to attack Diamond Island, situated within four miles of Fort George. In this expedition he failed. The artillery of the garrison

(1) — Quoted in Albermarle's *Memories of the Marquis of Rockingham*, (Vol. ii. p. 331) from the original manuscript in the handwriting of King George, now in the British Museum. This testimony seems to have escaped all of our American writers. The author's attention was directed to it by Major-General de Peyster.

(2) — See Chapter ix. on Ticonderoga.

was so well served that he was unable to come to quarters. The result we may give in Burgoyne's own words. He reports:

"On the 24th instant, the enemy upon Lake George attacked Diamond Island in two divisions. Captain Aubrey[1] and two companies of the 47th regiment had been posted at that island from the time the army passed the Hudson River, as a better security for the stores at the south end of Lake George than Fort George, which is on the continent, and not tenable against artillery and numbers. The enemy were repulsed by Captain Aubrey with great loss, and pursued by the gunboats under his command, to the east shore, where two of their principal vessels were retaken, together with all the cannon. They had just time to set fire to the other batteaux, and retreated over the mountain."

Colonel Brown regained Lincoln's camp in safety. He afterwards fell a martyr to liberty. He was a man of much character and ability, but he was kept from advancement by Arnold, who then had the ear of General Gates.

When Burgoyne was defeated and undertook to retreat, he started for Lake George, hoping to escape by this route to Canada. But the skill of Gates

(1)—Thomas Aubrey, second son of Sir Thomas Aubrey, of Glanborganshir, entered the army as ensign in 1762, and served in Florida. He was at the Battle of Bunker Hill, and was made major in 1782, and afterwards arose to the rank of colonel. He died January 15, 1814.

finally caused him to capitulate; and thus Lake George once more became absolved from British rule.

Nothing of importance occurred in this vicinity until 1780, when Sir John Johnson invaded the northern part of New York, and marked his track in ashes and flames. His object was to recover three barrels of silver plate buried in the cellar of his former mansion at Johnstown. He succeeded in finding the treasure, which was borne away by forty soldiers, each of whom carried a portion in his haversack. Sir John was pursued on his return by a force under Governor Clinton, who went down Lake George to Ticonderoga, where he was obliged to abandon the pursuit.

Major Carlton improved the occasion of this raid to strike a blow at Forts Ann and George. Fort Ann was taken October 10. The next day, Carlton, while marching against Fort George, was met by a party of twenty-five men sent from that place by the commander, Colonel Chipman, to obtain provisions at Fort Edward. They were immediately fired upon by Carlton, but managed to escape and return to Fort George. Chipman, supposing that it was an enemy's scout, sent out all but fourteen of his men, who met and engaged the enemy near Bloody Pond. The Americans were signally defeated, the whole force being either killed, wounded, or taken prisoners. Carlton then hurried to the fort, which was obliged to capitulate. The Americans lost twenty-eight men, eight vessels, and twenty-eight flat-boats, which were in the lake.[1]

With this event military operations on Lake George ended. During the war of 1812 they were not renewed, as at that time the lake had lost its importance as part of a great military route.

For the last eighty-five years Lake George has enjoyed all the advantages that flow from peace; and yet it still retains its native wildness. The lack of water-power and the lightness of the soil, retard the progress of mechanic and agricultural arts; and the shriek of the locomotive will perhaps never be heard around these shores. As this mountainous country will hardly require or admit the use of railroads, the stage-coach will hold undisputed sway, and, under a wise management, furnish to tourists, who pass by the Lake-George route to the Schroon Lake and the Adirondacks, a mode of transit that is at once easy, expeditious, and safe.

Lake George may therefore be considered beyond the reach of those invasions which have destroyed the value of so many American retreats. Elegant villas will multiply along its borders, and its romantic isles will, in course of time, be crowned with cottages; yet the visitor at the lake will never miss its old and exquisite charm, or fail to find retirement and peace.

(1) — Hough's Northern Invasion — Washington's Works, Vol. vii. p. 269.

TICONDEROGA.

CHAPTER IX.

Ruins! Ruins! Let us roam.

HOWE'S LANDING — THE FALLS — SITUATION OF THE FORT — NAME — ABERCROMBIE — AMHERST — ETHAN ALLEN — BEAMAN — ARNOLD — LOCALITIES — A TRADITION.

EVERYONE who visits Lake George will, of course, desire to see Ticonderoga. Landing at the north end of the lake where Abercrombie disembarked, a ride of four miles takes the visitor to the ruins of this celebrated fort, the examination of which, together with neighboring localities of interest, will consume a whole day. The Falls are well worth attention. The upper Fall is one mile, and the lower Fall two miles, from Lake George. About three-fourths of a mile from the fort the visitor comes upon the grass-grown outworks, which are numerous and complicated.

Ticonderoga was called *Carillon*, a French word, meaning a chime, the name being given with reference to the perpetual music of the Falls. The idea was suggested by the Indian name *Cheonderogo*, which in the Iroquois tongue signifies *Sounding Water*. The remains of the fort are situated on a beautiful peninsula, elevated a hundred feet above Lake Champlain. It is a position of considerable strength, being protected on three sides by water. It is overlooked, however, by Mount Defiance, which is nearly eight hundred feet above the lake.

The first attempt to fortify the position was made by Colonel Philip Schuyler, who arrived July 17, 1691, when on his way to attack the French fort at Laprarie. The weather being bad, his party remained here several days; and, being apprehensive of an attack from the enemy, they used the time in building a "stone fort breast high."[1]

Nothing more, however, was done until 1755. Twenty-five years before, the French had commenced the fort at Crown (Scalp) Point, where they evidently intended to establish the nucleus of a new colony; and at the above date the walls were in so weak a condition that Montcalm thought it advisable to advance to Carillon and commence an entirely new structure, instead of repairing the old one at the former place. Accordingly, he gave the proper orders, and the work was commenced, and by the close of the

(1) — Col. Doc., Vol. iii. p. 902. Palmer suggests that a fort called by Captain John Schuyler, "The Little Stone Fort," (Doc. Hist., Vol. ii. p. 62) was possibly built by Captain Sanders Glen, "while he was waiting there for the advance of Winthrop's army" in 1790. But a careful estimate of the distances will show that this fort could not have been situated nearer Ticonderoga than Crown Point.

year 1756, it was well advanced. They had also constructed three earthworks between the lakes. The stone fort on the east side was a star-shaped work, called Vaudreuil, in honor of the French Governor. From this time until the summer of 1759, the French labored continually to strengthen their works, which were spreading over a large part of the peninsula.

On Christmas Eve, 1758, Rogers and one hundred and fifty of his Rangers surprised the workmen, took several prisoners, and killed fifteen beeves. He wrote a note addressed to the commander, and placed it upon the horns of an ox for delivery. It is given in the Paris documents as follows: "I am obliged to you, Sir, for the repose you have allowed me to take; I thank you for the meat you have sent me; I shall take care of my prisoners. I request you to present my compliments to the Marquis de Montcalm." Some time after Rogers met M. Wolfe at Fort Edward, whither he had gone to carry despatches to the English, and the subject afforded some mutual pleasantry.

Baron Dieskau's troops stopped at Ticonderoga in 1755, when they were marching to attack the English; and also when they returned, broken and defeated. This was the rallying-point of Montcalm in 1757, before he moved against Fort William Henry. In July, 1758, it was attacked by Abercrombie, who was defeated with a loss of two thousand killed and wounded. Among the killed was young Lord Howe, a grandson of George I. When about to advance,

Major Putnam tried to persuade him not to expose himself; but he is reported as saying, "Your life is as dear to you as mine is to me — I am determined to go." He went.

Before Amherst advanced the following year, a party of Rangers attacked the workmen outside of the fort, and tried to burn the buildings, but failed. In the summer, when Amherst appeared with an army of nearly twelve thousand men, Montcalm evacuated the place, and retreated down Lake Champlain, leaving the English in possession.

After the defeat of Abercrombie in 1758, and while Lord Amherst was preparing to advance upon Ticonderoga, the French had a deep grave dug in the centre of their lines, over which was raised a lofty cross,[1] bearing a brass plate, with the following inscription:

" *Pone principes eorum sicut et Zebec et Zalmanna.*[2]

This was at once a braggart prophecy and a prayer, for which some over-zealous priest was probably responsible. But in the end they all found that Amherst was not exactly Abercrombie, and that he had not brought his army down Lake George to have it treated like Jabin at the brook of Kison, and like those who perished at Endor to fertilize the earth. Therefore when Amherst appeared, the soldier strapped

(1) — Warburton's Conquest of Canada, Vol. ii. p. 244.

(2) — "Make their nobles like Oreb, and like Zeeb: yea, all their princes as Zebah and Zalmunna." — Ps. lxxxiii.: 11.

his knapsack, and the priest packed his thurible, cope, and pyx, the latter leaving his litany to take care of itself. Indeed, Montcalm probably never intended to make a stand against Amherst.

Soon after the capture, Colonel Eyre planned another new fortification; but Colonel Haldeman, February 15, 1767, reported the works in a bad condition; and September 1, 1773, they were represented "in a ruinous state." Still, nothing was done, and the war of the Revolution broke out, finding them in the same dilapidated condition. For some time past the course of public events had led the New-England patriots to view Ticonderoga and its stores of warlike material with a covetous eye; and therefore when the time came for action they were ready.

At daybreak, on the morning of May 10, 1775, the fort was surprised and captured by eighty-five men from Vermont and Massachusetts, under the joint command of Benedict Arnold and Ethan Allen. The plan of this surprise was laid with secrecy and skill.

The person who claimed to be the first to entertain the plan for taking Ticonderoga, was one William Gilliland, who resided at Willsborough, on the west shore of Lake Champlain. In a petition to the Continental Congress, he says: "Your memorialist has reason to think, that he was the first person who laid a plan for and determined upon seizing Ticonderoga, Crown Point, and the King's armed vessel, and therewith the entire command of Lakes George and Champlain."[1] Yet this claim is put forth under circumstances that entitle it to little credit, and it can hardly be entertained.

The real originator of the plan was John Brown, Esq.,[2] a lawyer of Pittsfield, Massachusetts. As early as February 21, 1775, he received a letter from the Boston Committee of Correspondence, of which committee Joseph Warren and Samuel Adams were members, requesting him to visit Canada, and arrange for securing the co-operation of the people in the cause of Independence. In this mission Brown was unsuccessful, but he nevertheless wrote to the Committee from Montreal, saying: "One thing I must mention to be kept a profound secret — the fort of Tyconderoga must be seized as soon as possible, should hostilities be committed by the King's troops." He adds, moreover, "The people on New Hampshire Grants *have engaged to do this business*, and in my opinion are the proper persons for the job."[3] Here,

(1) — Watson's Champlain Valley, p. 175.

(2) — American Archives, Series iv. Vol. ii. p. 243.

(3) — Colonel John Brown was born in Sandisfield, Massachusetts, October 19, 1744. He graduated at Yale College in 1771, and afterwards practiced law in Pittsfield. He was at the capture of Chambly in 1775; also at Quebec when Montgomery fell. He was at the Battle of Bennington in 1777; and was killed, 1780, on his birthday, at the age of thirty-six, in Stone Arabia, New York, during the raid of Sir John Johnson. Forty-five Massachusetts men fell in the same action. But for the baneful influence of Benedict Arnold, whom Colonel Brown openly denounced, he would have been promoted at an early day.

unquestionably, was the beginning of a work which was positively to be done, in case of hostilities breaking out.

The next movement on record took place in Connecticut. April 27, in the morning, Samuel H. Parsons, of New London, while riding towards Hartford, met Benedict Arnold, who informed him of the amount of war material at Ticonderoga. On reaching Hartford he had an interview with Samuel Willis and Silas Deane, and at once decided upon action. Three other men were afterward joined to their number, when they drew three hundred pounds from the public treasury, promising to expend it for the use of the colony, at the same time making themselves personally responsible. The same day they despatched Captain Noah Phelps and Bernard Romans to the scene of the proposed action, having provided them with the requisite funds. After Phelps and Romans started, the Committee also engaged Captain Mott to go as one of the leaders. He left the next afternoon, taking five other volunteers with him. At Salisbury, Mott came up with Phelps and Romans, when eight new recruits were added to the company, which was all they then desired. Reaching Pittsfield the next Monday, they made known their business to Colonel Easton, and Mr. John Brown, in order "to take their advice on the same." It was, on consultation, thought best to begin to raise more men. Easton and Mott, therefore, started for Jericho, while Brown and the rest went to

Bennington. Wednesday, May 3, Mott also reached Bennington with twenty-four men. The next Sunday, May 7, the company united again at Castleton, the intervening time having been consumed in perfecting the arrangements.

In the meanwhile, Benedict Arnold had marched to Cambridge with a company from Connecticut. April 30, in reply to a letter of inquiry, Arnold wrote to General Warren, stating what he knew about the cannon and stores at Ticonderoga. The same day Warren wrote to Alexander McDougal, of the New-York Provincial Congress, saying that it had been "proposed" to him to take Ticonderoga. Three days later, the very day that Brown, Romans, and the others reached Bennington on their way to Ticonderoga, Arnold was commissioned by the Massachusetts Committee of Safety to raise men and proceed to take the fort in question. But without waiting to raise a man, Arnold started for the scene of action, as if informed by Warren of the action of Brown, and hoping, perhaps, to find a force prepared to execute his orders. He reached Castleton the day after the volunteers, who had already assembled, one hundred and seventy strong, and recognized Ethan Allen as their commander. Arnold at once applied for the command, by virtue of his commission, but his proposition, however, was spurned. He then started to overtake Allen, who had gone towards the lake. Subsequently, it appears, an arrangement was effected by which Arnold and Allen were to hold something like a joint command. In the meanwhile, the capture of Skenesborough was arranged for; and at the same time Bernard Romans, not being able to agree with the other members of the Committee, left them to go quietly, on his own account, and take possession of Fort George.

By the judicious course of Arnold, harmony was restored, and on the night of May 9, the whole party assembled on the lake at Shoreham, two miles below the fort, ready to embark and cross. But this proved a difficult movement, as the boats were not ready, and the wind was high. Arnold crossed with forty men and sent back the boat, which did not return until near daylight, being delayed by the storm. At this time there were only eighty-five Vermont and Massachusetts men on the west shore, and it was proposed to wait for the others. This was strenuously opposed by Arnold, who declared that he would enter the fort alone, if no one had the courage to follow. This had the desired effect; and when Arnold and Allen put themselves at the head of the party all were ready to move.[1] Ethan Allen claims in his Narrative, that he improved the occasion to extemporize a speech; but, however that may be, they soon dashed in at the entrance of the fort, where they found the sentry, who snapped his musket, and then attempted to escape. But he was soon made a prisoner, and obliged to lead

(1) — N. Y. *Journal*, August 3, 1775.

TICONDEROGA.

the party to the quarters of the commander, Captain De La Place. An eye-witness testifies that Arnold entered the fort first, though Bancroft simply says he entered with Allen, keeping emulously at his side. Allen beyond question demanded the surrender, though we may reasonably doubt his having used the language attributed to him. The astonished commander did not have time to dress himself, says the account, before he was summoned to surrender, "In the name of the Great Jehovah and the Continental Congress." Allen[1] professed little respect for the one, while the other did not then exist, the second

(1)—Ethan Allen was born in the town of Woodbury, Connecticut, in 1738. At an early age he settled on the New-Hampshire grants, now a part of the State of Vermont. When the troubles arose in regard to the jurisdiction of New York, he took a prominent part in resisting the law. He eventually became a sort of Robin Hood He was generous and beloved by his friends, but a terror to the partisans of New York. The authorities of that State proclaimed him a felon, and offered a reward of one hundred and fifty pounds for his apprehension. When the war of the Revolution broke out, he became prominent in connection with the capture of Ticonderoga, and afterwards used his influence to heal the dissensions between the States of New Hampshire and New York. The same year he united with John Brown, of Pittsfield, Massachusetts, in the attack upon Montreal, and was taken prisoner. He was held a prisoner until exchanged in 1778, but never afterwards performed any active service. From 1780, to the close of the war, his sword was sheathed. It is claimed that from this period he was engaged in a treasonable movement to attach Vermont to the King's government. At one time this was reported in England as accomplished. Allen died in Colchester, Vt., February 13, 1789, and was buried near Burlington. If we have left Allen less a hero than we found him, it is because the study of American history is now passing into a new stage, and it is not deemed necessary to engage in the indiscriminate praise of every person who happened to bear a part in the Revolution.

Continental Congress not assembling in Philadelphia until six hours after the fort surrendered; and a *week* after—when the news came—the members were on the point of apologizing for this hasty act. It therefore seems improbable that he used the language in question. The only person who had the semblance of official *authority* was Arnold, without whom the expedition possibly might have failed; and yet he could not alone command a bayonet. He was nevertheless recognized by the people, who, July 3, presented him an address conveying the thanks of the representatives of between five or six hundred families residing on Lake Champlain and vicinity.[1] Arnold's reply was written the next day at Crown Point.

It is worthy of notice, too, that the first person to receive public credit was Colonel Easton, who is represented in Thomas' *Oracle of Liberty*, May 24, as demanding the surrender of the fort. It is there stated that Easton "clapped him [De La Place] on the shoulder," calling upon him to surrender "in the name of America."[2] This of course is incorrect, yet the statement has a certain significance. The denial of Easton's claim was given, August 3,[3] by one of Arnold's friends, who, while declaring he was the first to enter the fort, does not claim any pre-eminence for Arnold as the originator of the plan. Speaking of the action of the Connecticut leaders, the writer alluded

(1)—N. Y. *Journal*, Aug. 3. (2)—ib. (3)—ib.

to simply says that Arnold "concerted a *similar* plan."[1] The statement that Arnold entered the fort in advance of Allen, has never been denied by any sufficient authority. Allen never claimed this particular honor, while Arnold reports to the Massachusetts Committee that he was "the first who entered and took possession of the fort."[2] And his statement will readily gain assent when we remember that Arnold was a person of unbounded assurance, and never allowed any man to go before him.

From this general statement of facts, it will probably appear, to unprejudiced minds, that the plan was originally formed by Mr. John Brown, and carried out by Vermont, Connecticut and Massachusetts men with Connecticut money. New York was informed of the design some days before, but gave no aid. Yet there were patriots who could applaud the act. Says one writer on this occasion: "The public spirit, prudence, and enterprising genius of the New-Englanders, will ever be admired."[3]

In this connection there is one other point that demands notice. Jared Sparks, in his life of Allen, states that he was guided into the fort by a young man named Nathan Beaman. This information, however, was received by Sparks verbally, through a second person, and he had no sufficient means of

(4)—N. Y. *Journal*, Aug. 3, 1776.
(5)—Force's Archives, Vol. ii. 557
(6)—N. Y. *Journal*, May 18, 1775.

investigating its truth. But Beaman[1] afterwards published what he calls a narrative, which shows a most remarkable degree of ignorance, and bears its own refutation on its face. The account given to Mr. Sparks states that his father was not acquainted with the ground,[2] while his published narrative states that he, with his father and mother, dined with Captain De La Place the very day before the capture, and that they spent the whole day on the grounds of the fort.[3] But what is more, he states positively that Arnold was not at the capture at all, and that "it was *some days* after the capture of the fort that Arnold appeared."[4] Such is the man whom Mr. Sparks brings forward to help make American history. Yet it is due to that eminent writer to state that he gives the source of his information in a note; and it would have been well if the popular writers who copied his statement had imitated his example, instead of lending themselves to the dissemination of a fraud.

According to his own finding, Beaman violated all the rights of hospitality; and one capable of such an act would not scruple to corrupt history. The most charitable thing, therefore, that we can say of Beaman

(1)—Beaman was a celebrated wolf-hunter, and was engaged in the "wolf frauds" of Northern New York.

(2)—Life of Ethan Allen.

(3)—See N. Y. *Spectator*, Feb. 7, 1847.

(4)—He also says that when Arnold appeared, he met Allen on the bridge, thrown across from Mount Independence to Ticonderoga, and that the latter knocked off Arnold's gold-laced hat, which sunk in the lake from the weight of bullion.

is, that he belonged to a class of men who for some years lived around the lake, cherishing prejudices that had survived the loss of memory, and all the while vaingloriously imagining themselves actually to *be* the heroes that, under favorable circumstances, they *might* have been.

By the capture of Ticonderoga, the American colonies secured what cost the British government eight millions of pounds sterling. A good morning's work!

The American forces held Ticonderoga until July, 1777. The New-York Committee of Safety had the cannon and principal war material removed up Lake George, while a portion of the light artillery was sent to Massachusetts. When the British commander, General Phillips, acting under the orders of Burgoyne, ascended Lake Champlain and took possession of Mount Hope, thus cutting off the retreat by the way of Lake George; and when General Frazer also began to erect batteries on Mount Defiance, the position of the American garrison became extremely dangerous. Accordingly General St. Clair, who was then in command, held a council of his officers and decided to order a retreat. At about two o'clock on the morning of July 6th, the Americans reluctantly began to file out of the works. Contrary to orders, some person set fire to a house, the light of which enabled the British on Mount Defiance to discover the movements. The forces were then obliged to hasten their departure and march with some disorder. The baggage was nevertheless got off to Whitehall, while the most of the troops took the road to Castleton, being pursued by the British. Thus Ticonderoga, though in a somewhat dilapidated condition, passed once more into the hands of the English. General Schuyler, then in command of the northern department, did not order this act, as was reported; while St. Clair himself was subsequently justified by an investigation.

September 25, Colonel John Brown, the author of the original plan to capture Ticonderoga, acting under orders from General Lincoln, marched with five hundred men and surprised and captured the outworks of Ticonderoga, with two hundred batteaux, an armed sloop, two hundred and ninety-three prisoners, and five cannon. He also released one hundred American prisoners, and recaptured a continental flag. Yet he did not, as on his first visit, succeed in getting into the fort, and was ultimately obliged to give up the attempt.

After the surrender of Burgoyne in 1777, the Fort was dismantled. In 1780 General Haldiman advanced with a few British troops and held the place. It was from this point that Major Carlton marched to attack Forts Edward and George, during the invasion of General John Johnson.

After the Revolutionary War closed, this structure, though built and maintained at an almost fabulous cost, was allowed to fall into decay. It is now a heap of mouldering and picturesque ruins, where the historian and antiquarian especially love to linger, dwelling in thought upon the olden times. Some localities and objects can be identified, while others must be left to conjecture. Let us, therefore, in imagination, take a stroll over the ground.

As we go up from the steamer's pier, we pass the old garrison well, and proceed on the same way taken by Arnold and Allen in 1775. But no drowsy sentinel snaps his fuzee as we enter the broken gate. Indeed, we can hardly tell where the gateway was. Nevertheless, we clamber over the fallen masonry until we find ourselves in the middle of the fort, and begin to look around us. Here, certainly, were the officers' barracks, where the high and massive walls now instantly threaten to fall. There is the entrance to the so-called "bakery." A poor oven, but a worse powder magazine, if the latter use ever claimed it. You must make your way into its dim recesses, and settle the question for yourself, remembering that when Amherst captured the place, it had *three* ovens or bakeries, instead of one.[1]

THE BAKERY.

(1) — Wilson's Orderly Book, p. 105.

The use of this open space we must certainly know. This is the parade:

> "The men at arms were mustered here:
> Here would the fretted war-horse bound,
> Starting to hear the trumpet's sound."

Up yonder, perhaps, was

> "The Lady's Chamber, whence
> With looks of lovely innocence
> Some heroine our fancy dresses
> In golden locks or raven tresses,
> And pearl embroidered silks and stuffs,
> And quaintly quitled sleeves and muffs,
> Looked forth to see retainers go,
> Or trembled at the assaulting foe."

We will say that Madame De La Place rested there. And this hole, which is now choked with rubbish,

> "Was the Dungeon; deep and dark,
> Where the starved prisoner moaned in vain,
> Until Death left him, stiff and stark,
> Unconscious of the galling chain."

At Crown Point the Jesuit Fathers had their Chapel and bell, and regular hours for prayer. It was undoubtedly so here at Ticonderoga. We may rightly find an ecclesiastical corner, and with our poet say:

> "This was the Chapel: that the stair:
> Here, where all lies damp and bare,
> The fragrant thurible was swung,
> The silver lamp in beauty hung."

There can be, however, no doubt about the kitchen, for all soldiers must eat, even if they do not pray or give thanks:

> "This was the Kitchen. Cold and blank
> The huge hearth yawns; and wide and high,
> The chimney shows the open sky."

And thus we might go on at any length, and spend the entire day in recalling the memories of the past. But the stage, or the steamer, we may fancy, is waiting to take us back to the landing at Lake George, or carry us down Champlain. Yet before you leave, visit the south bastion looking towards Mount Defiance, where tradition says that a beautiful Indian maiden once threw herself down headlong, in order to escape the importunities of a French officer, whom she had refused to accept as her lover. The tradition may not be a very ancient one, notwithstanding the fact that "we read in rare books"[1] of this occurrence; yet the summer tourist, who does not ask for historical authorities will not refuse a pretty embellishment of the local history. Besides, as all Indian localities can produce some legend of this kind, why should Ticonderoga fall behind the rest?

(1)—See Cook's Sketch of Ticonderoga.

SCHROON LAKE AND THE ADIRONDACKS.

CHAPTER X.

No chieftain raises to the sky
The gladness of his battle-cry.

Staging — Fort William Henry Hotel — The Route to Schroon — The Lake — The Road to Long Lake — The Lake System — The Mountains — Camp Life — Distances.

RAMBLING from point to point, we have now entered upon times of peace, and in our trip to Schroon and the Adirondacks, we shall have but little to say of the conflicts of former years. The new route to Schroon Lake and the Adirondack region, lies by the way of the head, or south end, of Lake George. The public conveyance is found in the coaches of the Glen's Falls, Lake George, and Chester Stage Company, whose lines are now in operation, summer and winter, furnishing an uninterrupted communication with Schroon.

The present points of departure are Fort Edward and Moreau, stations on the Rensselaer and Saratoga Railroad, only a short distance apart. The coaches from these two points unite at Glen's Falls, situated about six miles on the way. From Glen's Falls to Schroon, the distance is forty-two miles, the road running through a beautifully diversified country, whose signs of civilization gradually fade away, until they disappear in the mazes of the great wilderness of New York.

The proposed railroad, connecting the Saratoga road with Glen's Falls, will eventually make the latter place the great starting-point for Schroon and the Adirondack region.

In the opening chapter of this work, the route to Lake George has been briefly described; and since the road to Schroon passes the same way, it will not be necessary to speak of it again. Yet the lover of the horrible may be interested in viewing one locality not already mentioned, known as "Blind Rock." This rock, now sunk almost out of sight, lies a few rods east of the plank road on the side of the hill, a little beyond Glen's Falls. Tradition tells us that it marks "the spot where the eyes of captives were put out," and where, in the barbarous days of the early settlement of the country, "the Indian children set to amusing themselves by torturing them."[1] And if the visitor comes to Glen's Falls by the way of Fort Edward, he may not only view the site of that memorable colonial rallying-point, but may also get a glimpse of the grave of Jane McCrea, and the tree

(1) — Historical Sketch, by the Rev. A. J. Fennel, p. 6.

under which she is said to have been murdered by the Indians in the year 1777. Of late years the whole subject has been brought under searching examination, and the circumstances have at least been shorn of a portion of their romance; yet in all coming time this spot will possess a curious interest for the traveller.

The first stopping-place, after leaving Glen's Falls, is at the French-Mountain post-office and telegraph station, where there is a tavern known as the Half-Way House, midway between Glen's Falls and Lake George. Here the coach usually delays a few minutes; and the tourist, if he has occasion to do so, can step across the road to the telegraph office, and inquire the price of stocks on Wall street, or drop a word to a friend anywhere in the United States; or he may delay this act until he reaches Warrensburg, the terminus of the telegraph line.

Anon Jehu mounts the box, cracks his whip, and we are off on the firm plank road, which here makes staging so comfortable. In succession we pass Williams' Monument, Bloody Pond, Forts Gage and George; until finally the head of Lake St. Sacrament comes in view, with "Fort William Henry" Hotel standing on the site of the ill-fated colonial stronghold which bore that name. No one will think of riding by without passing some time in viewing the various points of interest, such as the Magazine, the Garrison Well, the Old French Burying-Ground, and the ruins of Fort George. Near the Lake House is the spot where Montcalm opened the trenches and planted his guns to batter down the walls of Fort William Henry.

The provisions made for travellers at Caldwell are ample. Built in the year 1855, and enlarged in 1856, Fort William Henry Hotel offers sufficient accommodation for three hundred and fifty or four hundred guests, whose comfort and convenience the proprietor has consulted by securing all those modern improvements and appliances found in first-class places of resort.

The village of Caldwell itself is pleasant, while its air is always salubrious. On Sunday, the church-going bell invites the traveller to the house of worship, and both the Episcopal and Presbyterian churches open wide their doors. The former church, being built of stone, is noticeable for its neatness; and, with the little stone church at Bolton, (built chiefly by the exertions of a young lady,) it forms the only representation of Episcopacy on the lake.

Monday noon, let us say, we mount to the top of the coach, (remembering that particular seats cannot be secured in advance, and that possession is even *more* than nine points of the law,) and thus we roll out of the village, passing on the right the Lake House, and on the left several small hostelries and stores.

The road to Warrensburg is somewhat wild and picturesque, and passes through dense forests of oak and pine. At Warrensburg we strike the Schroon River, flowing on its way to the Hudson, of which it forms a branch. A neat stone church, of the early English style, and one or two elegant private residences, here form the chief architectural adornments. This place is six miles from Lake George and about twenty miles from Moreau.

A few miles beyond Warrensburg, to the west, is Crane's Mountain, about three thousand feet high, noted for the profile of Washington formed by its being thrown against the sky. Passing on, over a road cut out of the side of a deep ravine, through which a stream is seen choked by boulders, and yet struggling on its way, the next village is Chester, twelve miles from Warrensburg, a little beyond which the summit of Landon Hill is reached, with its fine views of the surrounding country. Descending into the valley of the Schroon, at about six miles from Chester, we reach Pottersville. From Pottersville to Schroon Lake is nine more. At both Chester and Pottersville, the traveller will find good houses of entertainment; while at Schroon Lake a new and fine hotel has just been erected for the comfort of the constantly increasing throngs that now come to this charming place during the summer months.

Schroon Lake is a beautiful sheet of water, nearly ten miles long, situated partly in Essex and partly in Warren County. Properly speaking, this lake is an enlargement of the north-east branch of the Hudson

River. It stands much higher than Lake George, being no less than one thousand feet above tide-water. It contains but a single island, while the mountains around its border rise to the height of seven or eight hundred feet.

There is some difference of opinion in regard to the origin and meaning of its name. Spoffard says, that "a northern Indian, a tolerable English scholar," derived it from *Ska-ne-tah-ro-wah-na*, signifying the *Largest* Lake.[1] French writes: "Some say Schroon is derived from an Adirondack word," which means "a child or daughter of the mountain."[2] But a correspondent says that he once saw it stated somewhere, that the lake was discovered at an early day by several French officers from Crown Point, who were out hunting. They called it "Scaron," after the second wife[3] of Louis XIV. This correspondent also adds that a few years ago, "a Sappho-like origin of the name" was devised from "Scarona, a Squaw, who, like Winona and many others, had leaped over a

(1) — Gaz., p. 472. (2) — Gaz., p. 304.

(3) — *Francoise d'Aubigne Maintenon* was born in a prison, in Niort, France, November 27, 1635. She became a Roman Catholic, and was on the point of entering a convent; but in 1651, after a week's deliberation, married the comic poet, Scarron, who was both a paralytic and a cripple. She became a widow, October 14, 1660, and was greatly distinguished for her beauty. Her rare wisdom and wit attracted the attention of Louis XIV., who, unable to persuade her to accept any less honorable relation, made her his wife. After the death of the king, in 1715, she retired to the Convent of St. Cyr, where she continued to pass her days in charity and devotion, dying April 15, 1719.

precipice into the lake" and was drowned. But Governor Tryon's map of 1779, lays down the lake with the name "Scaron." The map of 1796 also shows this name. It is, therefore, not at all unreasonable to suppose that this lake, like Lake St. Sacrament, received its name from the French, who thus sought to perpetuate the memory of one of the most beautiful and distinguished women of those times.

There is considerable of interest to be seen here. For instance, on the north border of Chester is a natural bridge, under which a stream passes to Schroon Lake. This stream, after falling into a basin, enters a passage in two branches under the arch, which is forty feet high and eighty wide. It was described (1796) as running "under a hill, the base of which is sixty or seventy yards in diameter, forming a most curious and beautiful arch in the rock as white as snow. The fury of the water and the roughness of the bottom, added to the terrific noise within, have hitherto prevented any person from passing through the chasm."

The town called Schroon was formed from a part of Crown Point in 1804. The town of Minerva was taken from Schroon in 1817; and in 1840, the township still being considered too large, a part of it was re-annexed to Crown Point. The west and northwest portions are covered by the Schroon Mountains, and the northeast by the Kyadderosseras range. Mount Pharaoh is the highest

THE FALLS OF THE RACQUETTE.

peak of the latter range, it being no less than three thousand five hundred feet above the tide. There are numerous other lofty peaks that well deserve mention, and which well repay the tourist for climbing. Near Mount Pharaoh is a cluster of small but beautiful lakes, the principal of which takes its name from the great mountain by which it is overshadowed. Another of the lakes, near the centre of the group, is known by the name of Paradox Lake. The surface of this lake is so near the level of Schroon River, which forms its outlet, that during the spring floods the water flows into it, instead of flowing out. This whole region now made so accessible by the stage-coach, forms a charming place for a summer resort. But let us now turn our steps still further westward.

In order to reach the Wilderness region, it is necessary to retrace our steps to Pottersville, or else, when we reach this point in approaching Schroon, to diverge at once towards Minerva, leaving the jaunt to Schroon to be performed at another time.

The distance from Pottersville to Minerva, taking Olmsteadville on the way, is nine miles. Soon we enter the forest, and now, for a time, the bark shanty and occasional log house, alone tell of life. The road for a few miles is rough, but projected improvements will soon bring the traveller relief. The wild valley of the Boreas is erelong seen, and soon the rapid river itself is crossed. The Minerva road, at fifteen miles from that place, intersects the Carthage road, which runs through the wilderness east and west. Six miles from this point, and after crossing the Hudson, the traveller finds satisfactory quarters at the house of Daniel Bissell.

Thus far the road is, for the greater part, as good as the average of country roads, and continues such to the head of Long Lake, seventeen miles, near which, on the lake shore, is a thriving settlement, where good accommodations are found. Continuing thence, ten miles, and crossing the outlet of Raquette Lake, we come to a large house now open for visitors. We found that in passing on to Schroon Lake, we gradually rose eight hundred feet above Lake George, and during this stage of the journey, there is another lift of between six and eight hundred feet, which lands us upon the central portion of the great plateau occupied by the Wilderness of New York.

This region embraces a large portion of the counties of Warren, Hamilton, Essex, Clinton, Franklin, St. Lawrence, Lewis, and Herkimer. In the northern part of this tract are the Chateaugay woods. Contiguous to these are the St. Regis woods, which join the Saranac Lakes, and Raquette Lake. Away towards the east are the Adirondack Mountains; and on the south, Lake Pleasant and John Brown's tract.

There are four distinct divisions in the streams and lakes: the Saranac Lakes flowing through their outlets into Lake Champlain; Raquette Lake and its confluents flowing into the St. Lawrence; the head-waters of Black, Moose, and Beaver Rivers emptying into Lake Ontario; while the fourth finally unites in the Hudson and runs to the sea. This whole region is covered by a complete network of lakes, ponds, and streams, so that a large portion of the country may be

RAQUETTE LAKE.

traversed in boats. Yet in order to gain the fullest views of the scenery, it is necessary to travel more or less on land.

The magnificent sheet of water known as Raquette Lake, is seventeen hundred and forty-five feet above tide, in the northern part of Hamilton county. It is the geographical centre of the wilderness, and from the plateau upon which it rests, the waters of the Hudson, Black, Moose, and Raquette rivers, rise and flow in their several directions. This is the centre of the lake region. Raquette Lake is the largest of the interior lakes, and has a coast-line of seventy-five miles, of wonderful irregularity, forming projecting points and deep bays, which afford variety in every direction. The reflecting power of its pure water is remarkable.

To the east towers Blue Mountain, four thousand feet high, and directly at its base nestles that gem of the woods, whose charms are recognized by all—Blue Mountain Lake—the waters of which, after mingling with those of Eagle and Utowana Lakes, find their way through Marion River to Raquette Lake.

To the southwest of the Raquette, lies the Moose River chain of lakes, numbered from one to eight, the eighth of which is separated from west inlet of Raquette Lake by a portage of only one mile. These lakes extend through part of Hamilton and Herkimer counties, and can be traversed by boat twenty miles to Arnold's, on the Moose River, through which these lakes flow into the Black River. From Arnold's to Booneville on the Utica Railroad, land travel must be resorted to on account of the impetuosity of the river. Space will not permit even a notice of the lakes and streams tributary to this particular water system, and we can only say that the ascent of some of them would lead to places where the foot of man has never trod.

About four miles north of Raquette Lake, and accessible by the Carthage road, lies Beach Lake, noted not only for its beauty, but for preserving the name of the first hunter and trapper who made his home on Raquette Lake, at Indian Point. And it is worth while, perhaps, in this connection to state, that Mathew Beach, though possessing little book-learning, had, nevertheless, acquired a valuable kind of culture. He was a shrewd observer of character, and seldom erred in his judgment of men. He studied closely the habits of animals of the forest, and was a careful student of nature. In the autumn of 1861, while endeavoring (after a visit to his relations) to return to the forest home that he loved so well, Mr. Beach was overcome by the infirmities of age, and finally died in the month of March, 1862, at the "Lower Works," having arrived at the advanced age of more than eighty years. He will long be remembered by the earlier visitors as a good representative of the character revealed in Cooper's Leather-Stocking.

Raquette River leaves the lake of the same name, and after a northerly course of half a mile, enters Forked Lake, a large, picturesque sheet of water, having tributary to it a number of smaller lakes and ponds. Continuing its course from this lake, the river, after a succession of rapids and plunging over

Buttermilk Falls, enters and passes through Long Lake. This lake has been much and justly admired for its beautiful scenery. It is sixteen miles long, and its greatest breadth does not exceed two miles. Around its border high mountains rise in all directions. At its southern extremity is Owl's Head, with its craggy summit; and in the direction of its northern termination is Mount Seward. The river leaving Long Lake is broad and rapid, with but a single obstruction to boat-navigation for over thirty miles. At a distance of six miles are the High Falls, which are passed by a portage of one mile. About seven miles farther on, a diversion can be made through Stony Brook, a winding stream, and the ponds at its head, from which, over the Indian Carry of one mile, the upper of the three Saranac Lakes is reached.

And here once more we launch our boat on a beautiful miniature inland sea, where every prospect serves to delight the eye. The upper Saranac is the largest of the three lakes which bear this name. It is considerable longer and broader than Tupper Lake, and is, like the most of the lakes, beautifully studded with emerald isles. From this lake we may find our way to the St. Regis Lake; and, after viewing the scenery, work back to near the point of departure and then enter Round Lake, so called with reference to its shape, and cross to the mouth of the Saranac River. This stream empties into the Lower Saranac and passes out again at its side half way down. If bound for home, leave the lake where the river leaves it, and, following its course, make your next stopping-place at Baker's Inn. From this point, if there is time, travel by land on foot, or otherwise, to Lake Placid. Descending this lovely lake, overshadowed by mighty White Face, proceed to climb its sides. This done, we go back to Baker's, and thence, descending the Saranac River, emerge from the woods by the favorite route of Keeseville, Port Kent, and Lake Champlain. Otherwise, the Plattsburgh route may be followed, leaving the river at Bloomingdale, going by earth road to Franklin Falls, from the falls by plank road to Ausable Forks, and thence by carriage across the country to the place of embarkation on Lake Champlain. But *we* must go back another way.

Returning to Raquette River, at the point of digression, the tourist floats down the rapid current, around bends, over gravelly beds, along banks rich in varying scene and changing verdure, when all at once, by the stroke of an oar, and, as if by magic, the sight of one of the finest sheets of water in the world bursts upon the view. The effect of this sudden transition can hardly be described. This body of water is Tupper Lake, with its islands, overhanging cliffs, and rocky shores. A singular feature, and one without parallel in all this region, is the rushing of Bay River over a rocky ledge directly into the lake at its head.

Passing around these falls, and up a stream, which is sometimes so rapid as to enforce a portage of two miles, made along by the side of a succession of foaming cascades, Lake Clute will be reached. This is another large, beautiful, and picturesque body of water. Continuing through a series of small lakes, with occasional portages, the tourist again finds Beach and Raquette Lakes, having made a long and circuitous voyage. At Lake Clute an easterly course can be taken by way of Slim and Clear Ponds to Long Lake. When returning homewards we shall see that the west branch of the Hudson has its source in Hendrick Spring, within three-fourths of a mile of the east bank of Long Lake. Formerly the spring divided its flow between the waters of the Raquette and Hudson, but the hand of man has destroyed this beautiful feature. Following down the Hudson through Round Pond, Catlin Lake, Long and Lily Ponds, Lakes Rich and Harris, each with their peculiar natural charms, a point is reached just above the Carthage Road Bridge, where the east and west branches of the Hudson unite to form the noble river, which constantly gathers strength as it advances on its romantic but resistless course towards the distant sea. But we are to speak of the mountains.

Remarkable as is the network of this great inland lake and river system, so inadequately described, a field of interest, more wonderful if possible, is afforded in the lofty ranges, and in that august group of mountains, which testify of natures ancient, and mighty upheaval. Of the ranges, there are four: The Clinton, the Palmertown, the Luzerne, and the Chateaugay. These are parallel, nearly equidistant, and, having a north-easterly course through the heart of the Wilderness, terminate on the westerly shore of Lake Champlain. The Clinton range, the largest of these, is remarkable as furnishing at its most elevated position, a base for the lofty pinnacles known as the Adirondack group, the principal of which are Marcy, McIntyre, McMartin, Seward, (surrounded by *Cough-sa-ra-geh*—Dismal Wilderness), and Whiteface; the first being the highest in the State, having an elevation of five thousand four hundred and sixty-seven feet. At the point of intersection of the Minerva with the Carthage road, the visitor takes an easterly course along the latter for about a mile, to the "Lower Works," at the foot of Lake Sanford, whence a road of ten miles conducts to the Adirondack "Upper Works." From thence to Mount Marcy, or Tahawus, the Cloud-piercer, it is four miles, and three miles farther to the summit. The view to be had from here will repay the fatigue of the arduous ascent up the rugged, precipitous steeps. The term group does not fully express what might be called the personal characteristics of these peaks, towering in their solitary grandeur. Close by, between Wall-Face and McIntyre, is the Indian or Adirondack Pass, at an elevation of twenty-eight hundred feet above tide. This pass is a great chasm, one mile in length, produced by an ancient convulsion, and whose massive walls rise perpendicularly over a thousand feet. Besides those named, are Santanoni, Dix Peak, the mountains about Tupper Lake, Moose River Mountains, Blue Mountain, Goodenow, and many others having peculiar features of interest. The Carthage road, as it approaches Long Lake, passes at the foot of Mount Goodenow, south from which is Mount Joseph, bearing evidence of once having been a volcano. On the very summit of this mountain is a lake of great depth, whose boundary on one side is removed from the edge of the mountain but by a step, and at no place is the water-shed of sufficient extent to meet ordinary evaporation, while from the lake a stream of good size runs down the mountain side. Whence, then, comes the unfailing supply?

In this rapid survey of the mountains and lakes of the wilderness, the object has been not to undertake full descriptions which would require many chapters, but to give a general idea of the routes usually followed, and the principal objects of interest.

It is hardly necessary to remind the traveller that in entering the wilderness region, he will, in a great measure, leave civilization behind him. Indeed, it is hard to believe that so wild a region can exist within the boundaries of the State. Of villages there are few, and the loghouse, the bark shanty, and the tavern and the hotel, are the chief habitations that the interior region can boast. These, however, prove sufficient for the visitors who come here, and who take a peculiar satisfaction in overcoming the difficulties of living. Yet the foot-falls of a steadily marching civilization are heard with increasing distinctness every year, and the villages are rapidly extending their borders.

At Minerva is Champney's house. Eight miles beyond is Cunningham's, formerly Hewitt's. On the Carthage road, one mile east from intersection of Minerva road, is the Tahawus House, and one mile east of that is John Cheney's. Six miles west from the junction of the two roads is Daniel Bissell's, long and favorably known. At the settlement on Long Lake is the public house of C. H. Kellogg, and also the house of Mitchell Sabattis, extensively known as hunter and guide. Three miles farther, at head of the lake, is the pleasantly situated farm-house of Mr. E. Palmer. At Raquette Lake, the house kept by Mr. Cary. At the foot of High, or Raquette Falls, below Long Lake, is Johnson's. At head of Tupper Lake is the rustic cottage under the care of Mr. and Mrs. Graves. At the Saranac Lakes there are good houses which are easily found, such as Baker's on the Saranac River, Martin's on the Saranac Lake, Paul Smith's Forest Resort on the little St. Regis, Virgil Bartlett's, twelve miles from Martin's, and numerous others. But, Reader, if you go to the Adirondacks, do not give yourself too much care about such things. Whoever travels into the Wilderness region of New York for the sake of the hotels had better remain in New York. Rather, take your canoe and tent and trust to your hook and rifle. Here Izaak Walton would have gone into extacies, while, for ought we know, Nimrod, the mighty hunter, would have died for joy.

The fishermen and the hunters are indeed in their element. For the one, the lakes and streams are stocked with splendid fish, while for the other, the woods abound with every variety of game, from the wild-cat up to the deer, the moose, the wolf, the panther, and the bear. And as with beasts, so with birds. You may shoot the partridge or the loon, the eagle or the duck.

Until within a few years, this region was not often visited by summer tourists. A trip to the Adirondacks was viewed as something attended by great danger and incredible hardship. But now every season brings a great throng of nature-loving people from our large towns and cities, to rough it in the rude shanty, to sleep under white tents that dot the wide expanse of living green, and to broil the appetizing venison steak, with their own hands, over the embers of the evening fire.

On the border of this vast wilderness may always be found hunters and trappers who are ready to march away into the wildest recesses of the woods, and act the part of trusty leaders and guides.

The following table of distances will be found reliable; and by taking it as a guide, the tourist

ALBANY LAKE.

will be able to make the most of his time, and give the due proportion to every part of the work he has before him.

Lake George to Warrensburg,	6	miles.
Warrensburg to Chester,	12	"
Chester to Pottersville,	6	"
Pottersville to Minerva,	9	"
Minerva to intersection of Carthage road,	15	"
Thence to Daniel Bissell's,	6	"
Bissell's to settlement on Long Lake,	14	"
From Bissell's to the head of the Lake,	3	"
Long Lake to Raquette Lake,	10	"
From Pottersville to Adirondack,	22	"
" " " Newcomb,	28	"
" " " Long Lake,	42	"
" " " Roots,	18	"
" " " Elizabethtown,	41	"
" " " Keeseville,	62	"
" " " Plattsburgh,	76	"

At present the Glen's Falls and Chester Company carry passengers for the Adirondacks no farther than Pottersville. But thus far, at least, we have some of the best staging in this country. The coaches are all of the first class, and have skilful and experienced drivers, who are attentive and courteous, and always ready to promote the traveller's comfort.

From Pottersville a semi-weekly coach runs to Minerva; and from thence, once every week, an open wagon proceeds to Long Lake.

We wish you a pleasant journey and a safe return.

APPENDIX.

Appendix.

I.

ACCOUNT OF BERNARD ROMANS.

[MSS. in Connecticut State Library. Revolutionary War, Vol. iii. p. 26. Furnished by Charles J. Hoadly, Esq., Librarian.]

Colony of Connecticut to Bernard Romans, Esqr D^{r}. for monies advanced & for which he gave obligations, vizt:

To p^{d} Heman Allen going Express after Ethan Allen, 120 miles	£2.16. 0
To p^{d} Elisha Phelps ℘ rec^{t} on file . . .	30. 0.—
To p^{d} expences 3 Persons from Ben^{gtn} to Albany .	. 9.06
To p^{d} Benjamin French for Pork 4 bb^{ls} ℘ rec^{t} .	12. 0.—
To p^{d} Gershom Hewit Expence over lake . .	1.10.—
To p^{d} Jno Stevens Canaan, Expence ℘ rec^{t} . .	3.16.—
To p^{d} ditto d^{o} ℘ d^{o} . .	2.16.—
To p^{d} George Palmer Esqr for flower ℘ d^{o} . .	3. 1. 6
To my Expences at Albany	7. 6
To ditto, on road to Still Water, Fort Edward &^{c}	9.—
To ditto, at & near Fort Edward, getting men together	16. 4
To p^{d} Abram Wing in part for Expences . .	9.—
To d^{o} Cash to John Stevens	1. 8.—
To d^{o} horse-shoeing 7/6 —Expen^{s}, on road 5/- .	.12. 6
To p^{d} Butler for Expen^{s} as Express to Stillwater	.12.—
To horse hire for ditto	.15.—
To Expen^{s} on road at mead^{w} runbridge & Fort Geo: 16 men	1.10.—
To Expen^{s} on Lake & at Ticonderoga Landing .	. 7. 6

To d° at Ticond^a & on Lake returning	. 9. 4
To p^d enlisted men for their Exp^s. — Peter Caswel ℘ Rec^t	4. 2.—
To Expe^s on road & at Saratoga, returning . .	. 9.—
To d° at Lanesborough d° . . .	. 7.—
To p^d Mayhon Wagoner to Transport Prisoners from Lake to Lanesborough	2.12. 6
To p^d Prisoners Expences at Lanesborough .	.16.10
To fetching my horse rode by Jn° Brown, & keeping &°	1. 8.—
To advanced mony to one of Prisoners sick .	.12.—
To p^d for 10 Loaves Bread for Prisoners . .	. 7. 6
To 10^lb Pork for ditto . . .	. 5.—
To p^d two Waggoners from Lanesbor° to Nobletown 58 miles each — they found themselves	6. 0.—
To p^d Exp^s at Lanesbor° 5/– d° on Road 7/6 .	.12. 6
To p^d for Ton Iron to Mr French, for Chains .	28.10.—
To Expences advanced on the Road as ℘ Bill from Hartford to Bennington including a Gun bo^x for Capt Mott 50/– for which he must be charged & also 35/3 Expence paid for Mott	19. 8. 4
To Expences on the Road	1.16.—
	£131.11.10

SUPRA— C^r

By Cash rec^d of Messrs Deane Leffingwell &° ℘ Rec^t	100. 0. 0
By an order on Treasurer in full this acco^t this 31st day May 1775	31.11.10
	£131.11.10

Errors Excepted

℘ B ROMANS.

II.

PETITION OF JOHN NORDBERG.

[From N. Y. Miscellaneous Papers, Vol. xxxi. p. 15. N. Y. Revolutionary Papers, I. p. 206. In Office of Secretary of State at Albany.]

"THE MOST RESPECTABLE GENTLEMEN,
PROVINCIAL CONGRESS IN NEW YORK.

"I beg leave to represent to the most respectable Congress this circumstance.

"I am a native of Sweden, and have been persecuted for that, I have been against the French faction there.

"I have been in His Britanick Magesty's Service sinse January 1758.

"I have been twice shot through my body here last war in America, & I am now 65 years old — reduced of age, wounds & and gravels, which may be seen by Doctor Jones's certificate.

"1773. I got permission in Jamaica to go to London where I petition to be an Invalid officer, but as a foreigner I could not enjoy a commission in England, or Ereland His Magisty was graciously pleased to give me the allowance for Fort George 7 shilling sterling per day, with liberty to live where I please in America, because the fort has heen abandoned this 8 year and only 2 men remain there for to assist any express going between New York and Canada. I arrived here in New York last year in September with intention to live in New York: as I heard nothing els than disharmony amongst Gentlemen which was not agreeable to my age. I resolved to go to Fort George and live there in a little Cottage as an Hermit, where I was very happy for 6 months.

"The 12 of May last Mr. Romans came & took possession of Fort George, Mr. Romans behaved very genteel and civil to me. I told that I did not belong to the army and may be considered as a half pay officer invalid, and convinced him that I was pleagd with Gravell, Mr. Romans give me his passport to go to New Lebanon for to recover my health, & he told me that in regard to my age, I may go where I please.

" As I can't sell any bill for my subsistance, & I can't live upon wind and weather, I therefore beg and implore the most respectable Congress permission to go to England, and I intend to go to my native country, I could have gone away secret so well as some others have done, but I will not upon any account do such a thing — I hope the most respectable will not do partially to refuse me, because major Etherington, Captain Brown, Captain Kelly which is in the army have been permitted to go to England, and it may happen they return here again on actual Service, which old age & infirmities render me incapable of.

" As it is the custom among the Christian nations and the Turks, that they give subsistance to every Prisoner according to their Rank should the most respectable Congress, have any claim upon me to be a prisoner here, I hope they will give me my subsistence from th 12 of May last, according to My Rank as Captain I implore the favor of the most respectable Congress answer. I have the honour to remain with great respect,

" GENTLEMEN

" Your most obed[t] humble Servant

" JOHN NORDBERG.

" NEW YORK, decemb[r] 1775."

III.

LAKE CHAMPLAIN.

Lake Champlain was discovered and named by Samuel de Champlain, in 1609. It appears that he had left the infant colony of Quebec for the purpose of exploring the interior ; and having advanced as far as possible with his boat on the Richelieu River, he left the boat, and, attended by only two of his followers, joined a party of Algonquin Indians, who were proceeding in their canoes to give battle to the Iroquois. July 2, they travelled on foot around the Chambly Rapids, which had obstructed the passage of his heavy boat, the Indians carrying their light canoes. Re-embarking above the rapids, they sailed on until they emerged upon the great lake to which he gave his name, and then bore away southward up the lake, and met the Iroquois between Ticonderoga and Crown Point. The night previous to the battle both parties spent the time usually devoted to sleep in preparing for the encounter. This consisted in singing and dancing, and in applying to each other all manner of abusive epithets, accompanied by declarations of what on the morrow they intended severally to acchieve. Yet, as the Iroquois were unaccustomed to fire-arms, when the day came they were soon put to rout. Champlain gives the following account of the fight. He says :

" My companion and I were always concealed, for fear the enemy should see us, preparing our arms the best we could, being, however, separated, each being in one of the canoes belonging to the savage *Montagners*. After we were equipped with light armor, we each took an arquebus and went ashore. I saw the enemy leave their barricade. There were about two hundred men of strong and robust appearance, who were coming slowly towards us, with a gravity and assurance that greatly pleased me, led on by three chiefs. Ours were marching in similar order, and they told me that those who bore the three lofty plumes were chiefs, and that there were but these three, who were to be recognized by these plumes, which were considerably larger than those of their companions, and that I must do all that I could to kill them. I promised to do what I could, and that I was very sorry that they could not clearly understand me, so as to give them the order and plan of attacking their enemies, as we should certainly defeat them all; but there was no help for that; that I was very glad to encourage them and to manifest my good will when we should be engaged.

"The moment we landed they began to run about two hundred paces towards their enemies, who stood firm, and had not yet perceived my companions, who went into the bush with some savages. Our's commenced calling me in a loud voice, and making way for me, opened in two, and and placed me at their head, marching about twenty paces in advance, until I was within thirty paces of the enemy. The moment they saw me, they halted, gazing at me and I at them. When I saw them preparing to shoot at us, I raised my arquebus, and aiming directly at one of the three chiefs, two of them fell to the ground by this shot, and one of their companions received a wound, of which he died afterwards. I had put four balls in my arquebus. Our's, on seeing a shot so favorable for them, set up such tremendous shouts that thunder could not have been heard; and yet, there was no lack of arrows on both sides. The Iroquois were greatly astonished seeing two men killed so quickly, who were provided with arrow-proof armor woven of cotton thread and wood; this frightened them very much. Whilst I was re-loading, one of my companions in the bush fired a shot which so astonished them anew, seeing their chiefs were slain, that they lost courage, took to flight, and abandoned the field and their fort, hiding themselves in the depths of the forest, whither pursuing them, I killed some others. Our savages also killed several of them and took ten or twelve prisoners. The rest carried off the wounded. Fifteen or sixteen of ours were wounded by arrows, but they were promptly cured."

After this the party returned, and the savages amused themselves by torturing their prisoners, one of whom Champlain shot, in order to deliver him from his cruel tormentors. This was, undoubtedly, the first time that a white man ever saw the lake. In course of years, as seen by the history of Lake George, this lake became a part of the great route between the Canadas and New York.

As early as 1730, the French conceived the idea of founding a great political power on the shores of the lake, the capital of which should be Crown Point. Here they built a fort called Fort St. Frederic, and laid the foundations of an extensive settlement, of which many traces are still found by the antiquarian. Twenty-five years later, as the reader has already been informed, the fort was built at Ticonderoga. But in 1759 the French power on Lake Champlain was broken, and their plans and settlements were dissolved.

There were but few events in the history of Lake Champlain during the Revolutionary struggle, that are not detailed in the history of Lake George. The day after the capture of Ticonderoga, the fortress at Crown Point, garrisoned by a dozen British troops, also surrendered, and within a short time Benedict Arnold captured some British craft that were unsuspectingly abroad on the lake. Yet during the Revolution there was but little severe fighting here.

In the year 1814, Lake Champlain was made quite memorable in our naval annals by the victory of the American commander, Commodore Macdonough, over Commodore Downie. Macdonough's force consisted of fourteen vessels, eighty-six guns, and eight hundred and eighty men ; while Downie had sixteen vessels, ninety-five guns, and one thousand men.

The battle took place opposite Plattsburgh, on Sunday morning, September 7. Soon after daylight, the Americans had intelligence of the approach of the British, and the fleet was prepared for action.

Before the fight commenced, an unusual scene was enacted on board the Flag-ship Saratoga. Assembling his crew on deck, prayers were read by Commodore Macdonough, who fervently implored the Divine protection, and the successful termination of the conflicts, all the while the housetops on shore being covered by spectators, awaiting the issues of the day with the most painful anxiety.

When the enemy, with flags and streamers flying, came around Cumberland Head, and arrived within range, Macdonough sent a twenty-four pound shot the entire length of the deck of Downie's flag-ship, killing a number of men. The Americans then opened a general fire, which the English did not return until they were able to do so with great effect. At the first broadside of the English Flagship, the Confidence, a large number of the crew of the Flag-ship Saratoga were either killed or wounded. But the men rallied and gave a powerful reply, the broadsides being exchanged with such rapidity that the vessels at times seemed all aflame. Twice the cry was raised that Commodore Macdonough was killed, and it seemed at one time as if it would be necessary to surrender; yet by a skilful manœuvre the fight was maintained until the British commander himself was killed, and his colors pulled down.

The other vessels of the fleet were managed with equal gallantry, and the British were all obliged to surrender, with the exception of the small gun-boats, which, at the end of two hours and a half, escaped from the harbor with the aid of their sweeps.

While this battle was going on, the British were active upon the land, fourteen thousand men under General Provost attacking an unequal force of Americans under General Macomb. The result of the contest on the lake, however, disheartened Provost, who finally beat a retreat.

Thus ended a memorable struggle, rendered all the more interesting by the place where it occurred, which was not, like most naval engagements, on the dark, blue, boundless sea, but on this inland lake, bordered by hamlets, villages, and farms, and environed on all side by green hills, meadows, and distant mountains.

The people of New York and Vermont residing on the shores of the lake, thus found themselves at liberty to pursue their respective avocations until the war with England closed.

Lake Champlain is one hundred and fifty miles long, and varies greatly in width. Some parts being only a fourth of a mile wide, and others stretching out to a breadth of thirteen. It covers an area of more than five hundred square miles. Its water, unlike that of Lake George, is more or less discolored, especially on approaching the southern terminus, or South Bay, where the water becomes muddy. Here, too, the channel grows narrow, and at times the steamer glides along within a few feet of overhanging cliffs which lie on the east side; while on the west are the so-called "Drowned Lands," consisting of swamp and marsh. It was by this route that Burgoyne brought the bulk of his army in 1777.

Towards the north, the scene constantly improves; yet, nevertheless, we miss the sweetness and beauty of Lake George. We occasionally fall in with odd-looking craft. The number of vessels engaged in the navigation of the lake is not large, though their extremely picturesque character renders them objects of interest. Modeled often after the pattern of the Ark, or at least the Chinese junk, these clumsy craft — half French and half American, and ranging from thirty to a hundred tons, now sloop now schooner rigged, and now carrying the piratical latteen sail — go creeping at snail-pace from port to port all the summer, the domestic stove-pipe on the quarter-deck ever sending up its curling cloud-wreaths, and proclaiming the presence of the "skipper's" family, who, like himself, have a roving commission for the season, and no homestead, except that afforded by the surface of Champlain. We may also see rafts of canal boats from the ports of New Jersey that have come up the Hudson, reaching this lake by the Champlain Canal, on their way to Montreal.

In order to see every part of the Lake, the tourist must embark at Whitehall, where the steamers leave daily on the arrival of trains from Albany and New York, and proceed down the lake. After passing through what is known as the South Bay, and passing Ticonderoga, where the steamer always makes a landing, the lake begins to widen, affording a broad expanse of water, dotted here and there with islands; while in course of time the mountains rise in the distance on either hand; Camel's Hump and Mansfield Mountain looming up towards the east, and the cloud-splitting Adirondacks lying with especial boldness against the western sky.

Among the points touched on the lake, in addition to those already mentioned, are Chimney Point, opposite Crown Point, so called from the remains of French masonry; Port Henry a mile and a half north of Crown Point, on the same side; West Port, sixteen miles further on, lying at the east side; Basin Harbor, and Fort Cassin; the former five, and the latter eight miles from West Port. Cassin Harbor is named after Lieutenant Cassin, who, in 1814, defeated the British in their attempt to destroy the American fleet. Split Rock, on the west shore, near which is the lighthouse, forms the terminus of one of the ranges of the Adirondacks. Here a part of the mountain is split off, and separated from it by a chasm twelve feet wide, forming a very remarkable feature. Seventy miles from Whitehall, on the east side, is the city of Burlington, the seat of the University of Vermont. Port Kent, a small village, lies on the opposite side of the lake, which is now ten miles wide, and in the distance the Adirondacks appear. Port Kent is a point from which these mountains may be reached. At this place the tourist will feel repaid by delaying to visit the Falls and the Walled Rocks of the Ausable River, which, though comparatively unknown, afford some of the wildest and most impressive scenes to be found in the country. Everything may be seen in the course of a day. The next point of interest is Port Jackson, on the west shore, with Valcour Island opposite. Near this point, in 1776, Arnold was severely defeated by Captain Pringle, who commanded the British. On the same side is Plattsburgh, situated one hundred miles from Whitehall. Twenty-five miles further on, at Rouse's Point, we pass the American lines and enter the dominion of the Queen, where we at once begin to realize that we are in a foreign country. This is indicated by an occasional soldier in the Queen's uniform, and by the constantly increasing number of French Canadians of the lower classes, who, to their untidy aspect, add the equally poor attraction of their wretched *patois*. Here, also, the custom-house officials pay their respects to the traveller's baggage, and ply the question, "Anything dut'able?" The tourist may here go on twenty-three miles by water, or take train for Ogdensburg and Montreal.

MAP OF LAKE GEORGE.

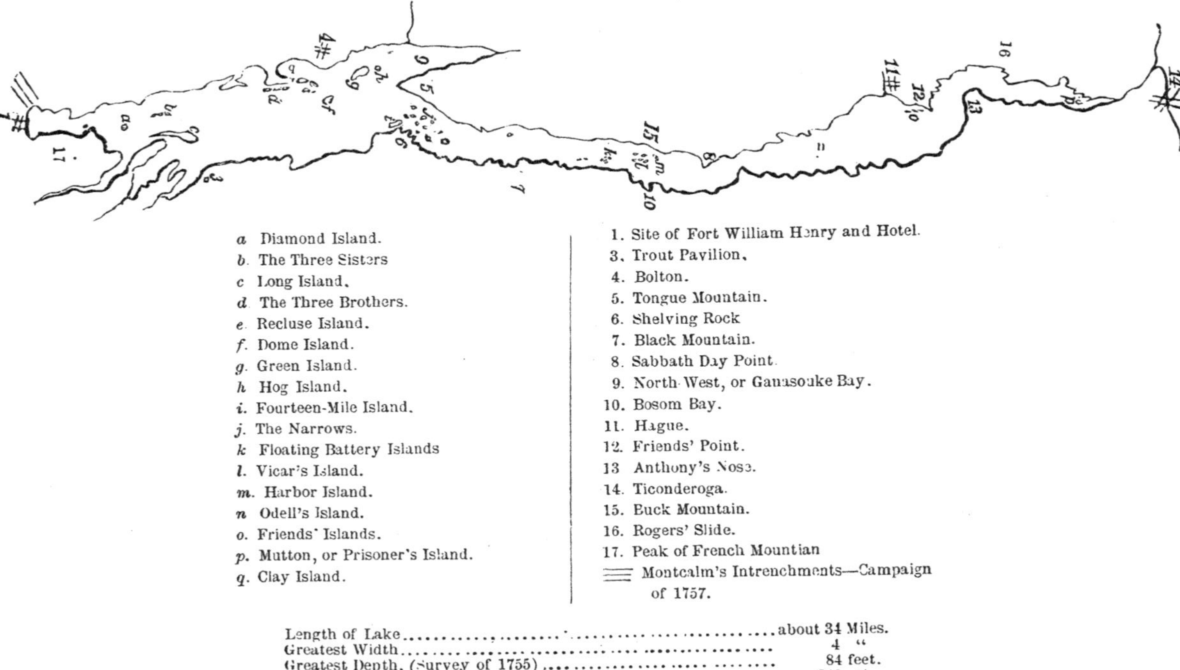

a Diamond Island.
b. The Three Sisters
c Long Island.
d. The Three Brothers.
e. Recluse Island.
f. Dome Island.
g. Green Island.
h Hog Island.
i. Fourteen-Mile Island.
j. The Narrows.
k Floating Battery Islands
l. Vicar's Island.
m. Harbor Island.
n Odell's Island.
o. Friends' Islands.
p. Mutton, or Prisoner's Island.
q. Clay Island.

1. Site of Fort William Henry and Hotel.
3. Trout Pavilion.
4. Bolton.
5. Tongue Mountain.
6. Shelving Rock
7. Black Mountain.
8. Sabbath Day Point.
9. North-West, or Ganasouke Bay.
10. Bosom Bay.
11. Hague.
12. Friends' Point.
13 Anthony's Nose.
14. Ticonderoga.
15. Buck Mountain.
16. Rogers' Slide.
17. Peak of French Mountian

≡ Montcalm's Intrenchments—Campaign of 1757.

Length of Lake..about 34 Miles.
Greatest Width..4 "
Greatest Depth, (Survey of 1755)........................84 feet.
Elevation above the Sea....................................240 "

www.ingramcontent.com/pod-product-compliance
Lightning Source LLC
LaVergne TN
LVHW011209110826
845150LV00006B/1379

* 9 7 8 1 4 2 5 5 1 7 9 6 0 *